COINS
AND
MONEY
TOKENS

COINS
AND
MONEY
TOKENS

Ian Angus

Ward Lock Limited · London

© Ian Angus 1973

ISBN 0 7063 1811 0

First published in Great Britain 1973 by Ward Lock
Limited, 116 Baker Street, London, W1M 2BB.

Text filmset in 11/12 point Monophoto Apollo by
Yendall & Company Ltd, Fleet Street, London.

Printed and bound by
'Editorial Fher SA Bilbao'.

CONTENTS

1
THE ORIGINS OF COINS

Whether we care to admit it or not George Bernard Shaw was stating the truth when he said 'Money is indeed the most important thing in the world'. It is impossible to imagine a world in which money did not play a part. Coins, as we know them today, have been in existence for almost three thousand years. Long before that – and right up to the present day in the more remote and un-civilised parts of the world – money took the form of various kinds of objects on which a value was placed. The earliest civilisations of the Middle East and the Mediterranean were pastoral, their wealth being in flocks of sheep and herds of cattle. Naturally, the earliest forms of money used by these peoples consisted of animals, meat and skins. Many of our words used in connection with money originated in this way. From the Latin word *pecus*, meaning a herd, we get the adjective pecuniary. The word 'talent', which now means an asset or a gift, denoted a sum of money in Biblical times, but long before that the Greek word *talanton* meant a cow-hide. When metal came to be used as money large pieces of copper

were shaped roughly like cow-hides to form money-talents.

The modern word 'bourse' is used to describe a place where merchants and businessmen meet to buy, sell and exchange goods. This is also derived from cattle, the ancient word *byrsa* meaning a cow-hide. Then there is the word 'salary', derived from the Latin *sal* (salt) – an allusion to the salt paid to Roman soldiers as wages.

Goods which were surplus to immediate needs have been used as barter coinage in many parts of the world. Bricks made from dried tea passed as currency in China and Tibet until fairly recently. Small cowrie shells (*Cypraea moneta*) were used as money in many parts of Africa till the end of the last century, and the first postage stamps of Uganda were inscribed with values in cowries. Until about twenty years ago potatoes were used as money on the South Atlantic Island of Tristan da Cunha. The *Tristan Times*, the island's wartime newspaper, bore the price in three different forms of currency – 3 cigarettes, 2 potatoes or $\frac{1}{2}$d. Wampum, shell discs, stone cartwheels and beads have been used as money in primitive societies, from North America to the South Pacific. In Europe at the end of the Second World War cigarettes were used as currency!

Money in metallic form began to appear during the early and middle Bronze Ages. Copper was worked on the island of Cyprus three thousand years before Christ, though it is not known when it was first used as money. In the ancient Greek culture based on Mycenae a talent of bronze weighed about 60 pounds avoirdupois. The talent used at the time of Homer was said to be made of gold, while the talent of the district surrounding Athens was silver and was divided into 60 minae, worth 100 drachmae each. These units of weight were widely used for bullion transactions throughout the ancient world in the pre-Christian era.

Copper in various forms has been used all over the world, from the massive plates of medieval Sweden to the crosses of Katanga in Central Africa and the manilla rings of Nigeria current until fairly recently. In Gaul and ancient Britain small bronze axes, known as celts, were used as a form of money. Similar objects, often elaborately decorated, were used in China and the Far East for the same purpose. Lumps of bronze, know as *aes rude* (rough bronze), formed the first coinage of the Roman Republic.

Crude iron ingots and bars were used as barter currency in Britain before the coming of the Romans and iron rods or spits formed the earliest type of small change in ancient Greece. The Greek word for a spit or dart was *belos* and from this came the word *obol* meaning a small coin. A handful of spits became a *drachma* – literally meaning 'a handful', but gradually came to mean a coin. The idea that metal can be equated with money dies hard, and survives to this day in such expressions as gold, silver, coppers, tin and brass to indicate money.

The various stages in the development of money were: 1, the barter of animals and hides, 2, then the use of copper and iron fashioned into rough objects and 3, the use of precious metals such as gold, silver or electrum (an alloy of gold and silver). It is not known when gold came to have a special value as a means of trade, but it was certainly well established in the Greek world by the tenth century BC and was regarded as being worth thirteen pieces of silver of equivalent weight, or 3,000 pieces of copper. Pure gold was not as popular as electrum, often described as pale gold or white gold. For centuries merchants were accustomed to weigh out the lumps of metal at every transaction, but gradually a more convenient system was devised. A rich merchant, or prince on whose land the metal was mined, would cast it into lumps of a uniform size and weight and guarantee the weight of these lumps by applying his personal stamp to them. At first this consisted of an irregular mark, made by striking the metal with a broken nail. The jagged edge of the nail left an individual mark which served to identify the person who issued the lump of metal. Sometimes these lumps had several marks struck on them in the form of a pattern. As a rule, the marks appeared on one side only, though the reverse side might have a pattern of lines, where the anvil had dug into the metal during striking.

According to the Greek historian Herodotus the Lydians were the first people to use coins. From the evidence of coin hoards and archaeological research it is now believed that the earliest coins of Lydia were produced in the middle of the seventh century BC. By 630 BC the crude nail mark had developed into a proper design, the lion's head emblem of the Mermnad dynasty. This emblem was applied to the obverse, or heads side, by placing the lump of metal (called the flan) on an anvil whose top had been engraved with the design. The flan, which had been heated until it was very soft, was struck by a hammer and impressed the image into the surface of the metal. At first the hammer had no mark on its surface, but gradually it became customary to include a simple geometric design which bit into the reverse, or tails side, of the coin. The earliest coins were either uniface (one-sided) or bore an incuse reverse (a simple design hammered into it).

Apart from their more elaborate appearance the earliest coins differed from the crude lumps used by the merchants, in that they were struck by the authority of the king or prince, and this came to be regarded as a guarantee of their value. The value of coins was still linked to the weight and precious metal content, but it was no longer necessary to weigh each piece at every transaction. Yet the age-old connection between weight and value has survived in many of our units of currency and measures of weight. The Latin word *pondus*, for example, has given us such words as 'ponder' – to weigh up, 'ponderous' – heavy, and 'pound', both a weight (lb) and a unit of money (£). The abbreviations for the pound weight and money come from another Latin word – *libra*, meaning a pound. This is preserved in the currency of many countries – lira (Italy, Israel and Turkey), or livre (France).

COINS OF
BIBLICAL
TIMES

Left to right:
Antioch stater of Augustus 27BC-17AD
(enlarged)
Lepton of Pontius Pilate 26-36AD
Bronze coin of Herod the Great 37-4BC
Shekel of Bar-Kokhba 133AD
Earliest Hebrew coin struck in Judea, 4th
century BC

2
GREEK COINS

Until recent years scholars believed that coinage was invented in the eighth century BC, but as a result of recent archaeological discoveries this date is now placed at about 650 BC. It is still agreed, however, that Lydia, a kingdom on the western seaboard of modern Turkey, deserves the credit for producing the first coins. The custom spread rapidly to the Greek cities dotted along the coast of Asia Minor. These cities were important commercial ports, through which much of the trade of the ancient world passed, and therefore the convenience of transferring wealth in the form of coins was quickly appreciated by the cities' tradesmen. Coins in those days did not serve the same purpose which they do today. It would be more realistic to regard these early pieces as precious metal ingots – convenient for storing wealth but not actually used as loose change.

Even the smallest gold or electrum coin of that period would have represented riches beyond the dreams of most ordinary people. The bulk of small transactions continued to be by barter as before. Two or three centuries elapsed before silver and bronze coins of a low face value were minted for ordinary commercial purposes and even then many people would seldom have the opportunity or necessity to handle coins in everyday life. This may explain why so many ancient Greek coins have survived in such good condition. Had they been subjected to the wear and tear of passing from hand to hand and jingling together from pocket to purse, as our modern coins do, they would not have lasted so well.

Among the early cities to issue their own coins were Abydus, Chios, Miletus and Phocaea. These coins are all exceptionally rare and valuable, but they are of great interest. The coins of Phocaea depicted a seal (in Greek *phoke* – a punning allusion to Phocis, the district of mainland Greece which colonised Phocaea). Chios depicted the sphinx on its coins, while Miletus featured a winged man-bull. Though some attempt was being made to place the civic emblem on the coins the reverse was left plain or bore an incuse mark, and no form of inscription was worked into the design. A notable exception was the stater (2-drachmae coin) minted by Phanes which not only showed a stag but bore the Greek words 'I am the badge of Phanes'. An inscription was quite superfluous since the emblem served to identify the coin well enough.

The striking of coins spread from Asia Minor to mainland Greece in the second half of the seventh century BC. Legend has it that the island of Aegina, conquered by Pheidon, king of Argos, produced the first coins of Greece itself. The fourth century historian Heracleides records that Pheidon abolished the iron spits previously used as currency and minted silver drachmae and obols bearing the leather-backed turtle, the symbol of Aegina. At that time Aegina was an important trading centre and soon the Aeginetan turtles, as these coins were called, were circulating all over the Greek world. On the reverse side they had a curious incuse mark which resembled the Union Jack.

Nearby Corinth soon followed Aegina and struck drachmae showing the famous winged horse Pegasus. Beneath the horse's belly appeared the obsolete Greek letter *koppa* (like our letter Q) which at one time was the initial for Corinth. The incuse mark on the Corinthian 'foals', as these coins were commonly named, resembled a swastika, the ancient symbol of good luck, or a clockwise arrangement of four triangles. Similar coins, though not so finely made, were produced by the Corinthian colonies in north-western Greece.

Corinth: Pegasus

The greatest of the Greek cities, then as now, was Athens. The Athenians were decisively defeated by the Aeginetans in 665 BC and did not recover their prosperity for almost fifty years. Athens was fortunate in having its own rich silver mines and from the beginning of the sixth century BC Athenian coinage gradually dominated the Greek world. The earliest Athenian coins were quite thick and featured an amphora or wine vessel. For much of the sixth century Athens was governed by various wealthy families and they put their own heraldic emblems on the coins during their period in power. Then, in 566 BC,

Pamphylia: Aspendus 4th century B.C. silver stater

Pisistratus came to power and founded the Panathenaean Games in honour of Athena, patron goddess of the city. At the same time he introduced coins bearing a profile of Athena on the obverse and showing a little owl on the reverse. The Athenian 'owls' were the first coins to have a proper design on both sides. For good measure the name of the city also appeared in an abbreviated form (*Athe*). Apart from short periods the Athena and owl pattern continued to be used on the coins of Athens right up till the early Christian era, but by that time the coins were struck in bronze and were permitted by the Romans for local circulation only. The later Athenian coins became increasingly elaborate, though the basic design of Athena and her owl remained. Many of the later coins had detailed inscriptions giving the names of magistrates and moneyers under whose authority the coins were struck.

Corinth soon copied Athens and produced coins with Pegasus on one side and the goddess Athena on the other. Similar coins, but with an identifying initial, were used in the Corinthian colonies from about 480 BC onwards. During this period many of the smaller towns and cities of Greece produced their own coins, particularly after the defeat of Athens at Aegospotami in 405 BC. For a time Athenian owls were replaced by the coins of the individual cities. Many of these coins were attractive and interesting and thus the era from 404 to 336 BC is often referred to by collectors as the finest art period. This was the period when beautiful coins were minted by Sicyon (Chimaera and dove), Olympia (Zeus and Hera), the Maritime League (Hercules strangling the serpents), the Boeotian League (shield), the Arcadian League (Zeus and Pan), the Achaean League (Artemis), and the Chalcidian League (Apollo). The cities of the various leagues and confederations usually featured the emblem of the league on the obverse while depicting their individual civic badges on the reverse, so that a wide variety of different coin types resulted.

Outside Greece proper many handsome coins were produced by the Greek colonies in southern Italy (Magna Graecia) and Sicily. These colonies were often as rich and powerful as their mother states, and were not slow in adopting coinage of their own. Naxos in Sicily followed Athens by producing coins with a design on both sides, featuring the god Dionysus and a bunch of grapes respectively. Other Greek colonies which had distinctive coinage in the second half of the sixth century BC were Himera (cock), Selinus (*selinon* or

Sicily: Messana 461-396
B.C. silver tetradrachm

Acragas, late 6th century
B.C. silver didrachm

wild celery) and Acragas (eagle and crab).

The most important of the Greek colonies in Sicily was Syracuse, most of whose coins featured horsemen and chariots or a profile of Arethusa surrounded by dolphins. Syracuse minted a wide range of coins, from the tiny obol (sixth of a drachma) to the tetradrachm (four-drachmae piece). After Syracuse won its independence from Athens in 413 BC an annual festival, known as the Assinarian Games, was instituted and special ten-drachmae coins were struck as prizes. The Syracusan dekadrachms of the fourth century BC are regarded as some of the finest coins ever struck. On the obverse they showed a quadriga, or four-horse chariot, while Arethusa and her dolphins graced the reverse. An interesting point about these coins is the appearance on them of the initials of the men who engraved the dies for them – Euainetos and Kimon – who have thus come down to us as the first recorded coin engravers and medallists.

In Magna Graecia the Athenian and Corinthian colonies produced very distinctive coins, both in design and in the technique used to strike them. Very thin flans were used and some kind of hinged dies, so that the same design appeared on both sides, but in relief on the obverse and

intaglio on the reverse. Numismatists have long been intrigued by these curious coins and speculated on the exact method used to strike them so accurately. The towns using these unusual double designs were Croton (tripod), Caulonia (Apollo), Metapontum (ear of barley), Sybaris and Pyxus (backward-glancing bull), Tarentum (Apollo and lyre, or Phalanthus riding on a dolphin), Rhegium (man-faced bull) and Zancle (dolphin). Of these, the coins of Tarentum enjoyed the longest life and widest popularity. The double types gave way to a reverse type showing a man on horseback. The 'horsemen' of Tarentum circulated widely all over the Mediterranean area and were the most popular coins in Italy until the Roman Republican issues in the third century.

No living person was portrayed on the coins of ancient Greece. The nearest thing to this was the horseman featured on the reverse of the tetradrachms minted by Philip of Macedon in the fourth century BC. The coin was inscribed 'of Philip', inferring that the horseman was Philip himself. Under his illustrious son, Alexander the Great, the Greek states were amalgamated with Macedon and became the heart of a great empire stretching from the Danube to India and Egypt. Alexander standardised the minting of coins

Philip II of Macedon

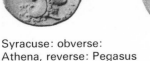

Syracuse: obverse:
Athena, reverse: Pegasus

Alexander the Great

Syracuse: silver
decadrachm obverse:
Arethusa, reverse: Victory
in quadriga

Lysimachus of Thrace

throughout his vast dominions in twenty imperial mints. Gold staters and double staters, and silver tetradrachms and smaller coins were given uniform designs with such well-kown subjects as Athena, Zeus and Hercules. After Alexander's sudden death in 323 BC his generals divided the empire among them, but continued to pay tribute to Alexander's memory by striking coins bearing his profile. On these coins Alexander was shown with the horn of Mammon sprouting from his forehead, to indicate that he had been elevated to the status of a god.

The Alexandrine generals founded their own dynasties and carved out the so-called Hellenistic kingdoms – Macedonia, Syria, Egypt, Thrace, Parthia and the Seleucid Empire. At first they continued to strike Alexandrine coins but gradually they introduced their own distinctive designs. Latterly several of these rulers placed their own profile on their coins and many of these coins are excellent examples of portraiture – particularly those of Perseus of Macedonia, Mithridates II of Parthia and the rulers of Egypt. It is interesting to note that Cleopatra was far from beautiful – if the beaky profile on her coins is anything to go by!

Even after the Romans had crushed the last of the Hellenistic kingdoms and established an empire stretching from the Clyde to the Nile, Greek coinage continued to appear. Certain towns were permitted to strike coins for local usage. They included Athens, Sparta (which had scarcely bothered to issue its own coins while it was an independent state), Nicaea, Syedra and Rhodes. The small bronze coins were rather like the traders' tokens mentioned in Chapter 11. They did not enjoy the wide currency of the imperial coins and were intended mainly as small change circulating locally. Nevertheless, in their excellent designs, they preserved something of the traditional qualities of Greek coinage and survived as late as AD 268. By that time the value of the Roman imperial coinage itself had become so much lower that there was no longer any need for a purely local bronze coinage.

Mithradates the Great

Ptolemy I of Egypt

Ancient Greece: tetradrachm of Lysimachus showing Alexander the Great (obverse) and Zeus (reverse)

Demetrius Poliorcetes of Macedon

Seleucus I of Syria

Rhodes: late 4th century B.C. Sun-god Helios

A Roman temple in ancient Corinth

3 ROMAN COINS

It is surprising that the Romans were so late in copying the coins of the Greeks. A mint for the striking of coins in bronze, silver and gold was established at Rome in 269 BC and it is usual to date Roman coinage from that year. Some form of coinage, however, was in existence several years earlier. At the beginning of the third century BC the Romans were still using crude lumps of bronze (*aes rude*) which had to be weighed out at each transaction. Gradually these lumps were replaced by bars and ingots of a uniform shape and weight. These ingots were known as *Aes signatum* – signed bronze – because they bore the stamp of the issuing authority on both sides. Significantly one of the symbols found on these pieces was a bull – a reference to the importance of cattle as a form of money in earlier times.

After *Aes signatum* came *Aes grave* (heavy bronze) – pieces which were cast in circular disc-shape not unlike coins, though very much heavier. The unit of weight was the *As* weighing a pound (*libra*) and bearing the Roman numeral I. Half of this was the *Semis* indicated by the letter 'S'. A third of an As was the *Triens* which, being worth four Roman ounces, bore four little pellets to indicate the weight and value. Smaller units were the *Quadrans* (fourth . . .), *Sextans* (sixth . . .) and the *Uncia* (ounce, indicated by one pellet like a

full stop). This heavy bronze currency first appeared in 269 BC but at the same time a series of silver coins was released, consisting of various types of didrachms (two-drachmae pieces) and their smaller sub-divisions of litra, half litra and silver as. Ten asses of silver or bronze were worth one silver didrachm. These silver coins bore the words ROMA or ROMANO (an abbreviated form of 'of the Romans'). The silver coins were strongly influenced in weight and design by those of the Greek colonies in southern Italy. They featured the Roman gods and goddesses – Mars, Minerva and Janus among others.

The political upheavals and wars of the third century had a harmful effect on the coinage of Rome. The bronze coins were successively reduced in weight, until eventually the bronze as weighed no more than the original 'uncia'. Gold coins were struck in 216 BC, as a makeshift, during a temporary shortage of silver as a result of the wars with Carthage. During the Punic Wars a small silver coin, equivalent to the Greek drachma, was minted and became known as a Victoriate, on account of the figure of Victory which appeared on the obverse.

After the defeat of Carthage Rome emerged as the most powerful state in the western Mediterranean and entered a new era of prosperity. The coinage was reformed in 211 BC and based on the silver 'denarius' – forerunner of the deniers and dinars used by many European and Asiatic countries in more recent times and preserved in British currency until recently in the symbol '*d*' to denote the penny. The denarius was divided into the 'quinarius' (five asses) and the 'sestertius' (two and a half asses). A board of moneyers, consisting of three officials elected annually, was created and henceforward their names, initials or family emblems began to appear on the coins, thereby assisting in the accurate dating of Roman republican coins. Roman coins became more and more elaborate in design. The most popular subjects were profiles of Roma and Bellona on the obverse and the heavenly twins, Castor and Pollux on the reverse. Bronze coins, from the 'as' to the 'semuncia' (half ounce), continued to be minted.

From 146 BC, when Carthage was finally destroyed, Rome expanded rapidly acquiring territory in North Africa, Gaul (modern France) and Iberia (Spain), suppressing the Greek colonies in southern Italy and advancing into the Balkans. The coins of this period had triumphant designs, featuring Victory, Mars and Jupiter on the obverse and elaborate designs illustrating characters and events from classical mythology. In 124 BC the

Claudius aureus (46 A.D.)
reverse shows a triumphal
arch symbolising the
conquest of Britain

Hadrian bronze sestertius
(117–38 A.D.)

Vespasian coin celebrating
the conquest of Judaea

brothers Gaius and Tiberius Gracchus reformed the currency on the basis of the denarius of sixteen asses. The coins became even more varied and interesting as each group of moneyers vied with its predecessors in incorporating emblems and events alluding to their illustrious ancestors. Many of these subjects are rather obscure and require a very thorough knowledge of Roman history and folklore to understand the meanings of the inscriptions and scenes.

No living person was portrayed on Roman coins at this time, though gradually the profiles of famous ancestors were depicted. During the first century BC more emphasis was laid on personalities and less on symbolism, at a time when Rome was dividing into political factions and cliques under such men as Marius, Sulla, Pompey the Great and Julius Caesar. Caesar struck gold and silver coins during his campaigns in Gaul and went so far as to place his age (indicated by the Roman numerals

LII) on his coins – one of the earliest attempts at putting a 'date' on coins. After 49 BC, when Caesar crossed the Rubicon, defeated Pompey and made himself master of Rome, his coins took on a more personal note. The symbols of liberty, justice and concord which hitherto graced the coins gave way to Caesar's personal attributes. They bore lengthy inscriptions referring to his various public appointments – Consul, Dictator, Pontifex Maximus (chief priest), Imperator (commander in chief, not emperor, as it later became) and finally Parens Patriae – father of his country. The last coins issued under Caesar's authority actually bore his portrait.

From Caesar's assassination in 44 BC to the battle of Actium in 31 BC was a period of civil wars, marked by coins struck on behalf of Brutus, Cassius, the sons of Pompey, the triumvirate of Mark Antony, Lepidus and Octavian, and finally for Octavian himself, after he had assumed the

Carausius denarius (286–293 A.D.) obverse Carausius, reverse galley

Carausius antoninianus of the London mint

Constantine the Great reduced follis (306–337 A.D.)

title Augustus and set about transforming Rome into an Empire. The first century BC was also marked by Roman expansion into the former dominions of Alexander and one by one the Hellenistic kingdoms were absorbed. The defeat of Antony and Cleopatra at Actium completed the establishment of the Roman Empire.

Four years elapsed before Octavian completed the change from republican to imperial government. In 27 BC he resigned his dictatorial powers and accepted the title of emperor, though he continued to renew his title every five years, down to his death in AD 14. Augustus Caesar instituted a new system of coinage based on the gold 'aureus' equal to 25 silver denarii. Lesser denominations included the 'quinarius aureus' ($12\frac{1}{2}$ denarii), the silver quinarius ($\frac{1}{2}$ denarius) the brass sestertius ($\frac{1}{4}$ denarius), the 'dupondius' ($\frac{1}{2}$ sestertius or 2 copper asses) and the as divided into four 'quadrantes'. Though the weights and sizes of these coins varied, the different denominations remained in use for most of the Roman Imperial period. The double-denarius, or 'antoninianus', was introduced in 214 BC under Caracalla. Apart from its size it may be recognised by the profile of the emperor with a sunray crown. As inflation overtook the Roman Empire in the third century AD the denarius and its lesser divisions disappeared and the antoninianus became the basic unit. The silver content of this coin was frequently diluted with copper and eventually it became a copper coin with a thin silver wash which soon wore off.

Under Diocletian important political and economic reforms were introduced in 295 BC. A new system of coinage was adopted, retaining the aureus and the denarius, but adding a new coin called the 'follis'. Twenty years later a new gold coin, the 'solidus', was issued. It was smaller than the aureus and gradually replaced it. From the

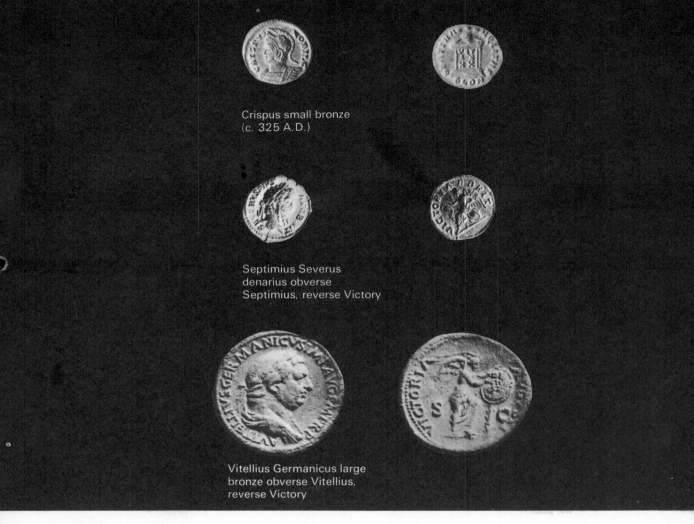

Crispus small bronze
(c. 325 A.D.)

Septimius Severus
denarius obverse
Septimius, reverse Victory

Vitellius Germanicus large
bronze obverse Vitellius,
reverse Victory

solidus is descended a whole host of European coins – soldo, sol, sou and the abbreviation 's' which used to denote a shilling in British currency. In the middle of the fourth century two new silver coins, the 'miliarensium' and the 'siliqua', were added to the range of Roman currency and finally the 'tremissis', a gold coin worth a third of a solidus, appeared about AD 410 when the Roman Empire was beginning to break up.

The subjects shown on coins in the Roman imperial period are of the greatest interest to the historian. Not only did the emperor enjoy the privilege of issuing coins, but numerous members of his family also struck their own coins. Thus we have a great galaxy of portraits, many of which were more realistic than flattering. The reverse side of coins bore mythological figures, allegorical subjects such as peace, justice, liberty and harmony. In the fourth century there were large

brass coins struck to commemorate outstanding events, such as the eleventh centenary of Rome, celebrated in AD 348. Famous buildings and historic landmarks were often featured on these large, handsome coins.

The rapidly spreading influence of Christianity in the Roman Empire led to the appearance of the XP (chi-rho) monogram of Christ on the coins struck by Magnentius in AD 350. The inscriptions on Imperial coins became exceedingly long and wordy, though the titles of the emperor, empress or member of the imperial family were usually abbreviated in order to cram as much as possible into the space allotted. After the name of the emperor, for example, would come such abbreviations as IMP (Imperator) CAES (Caesar) AVG (Augustus), PM (Pontifex Maximus), TRP (Tribunician Power), COS (Consul) and PP (Parens Patriae). Sometimes Roman numerals were added to the lesser titles indicating in which year of office the coin had been struck. At various times there was more than one emperor, and sometimes as many as four sharing the imperial power. This would be indicated by repeating the G of AVG to the requisite number. Thus coins of Carausius bore the abbreviation AVGGG, in recognition of the position of Diocletian and Maximian as co-emperors. Other abbreviations found on Roman coins include EX S.C. (From the Senate in consultation) REST (*restituit* = restored) and SPQR (the Senate and People of Rome). Some of the emperors also had nicknames like *Divus* (god-like), *Felix* (lucky) or *Rector orbis* (ruler of the world).

In AD 364 Valentinian divided the empire into eastern and western provinces, assigning the eastern empire to his brother Valens. From that time there were two Roman empires, based on Rome and Byzantium (Constantinople) respectively. The western empire came to an end in AD 476 when the last emperor Romulus Augustus was defeated by the Ostrogoths. The Ostrogothic king Theodoric minted coins with his portrait on one side and a figure of Rome on the other, with the caption *Invicta Roma* (unconquered Rome). These coins were crude in comparison to the classical issues and they form an ironic tail-piece to seven centuries of Roman coinage. In the east the Roman empire survived a further thousand years, until the capture of Constantinople by the Turks in 1453. The coins of the Byzantine Empire followed Roman traditions. An interesting feature, however, was the portrayal of the emperor full-face and the inclusion of Christ and the Virgin Mary together with other Christian symbolism. Unfortunately the quality of engraving on Byzantine coins deteriorated over the centuries as the old standards of the Roman Empire declined.

Antoninus Pius sestertius (138–61 A.D.) showing Britannia

A Roman Centurion

THE TWELVE CAESARS

Julius Caesar

Representative selection of Roman Imperial coins portraying the Twelve Caesars.

Augustus

Tiberius

Caligula

Claudius

Nero

Galba

Otho

Vitellius

Vespasian

Titus

Domitian

4 MEDIEVAL EUROPEAN COINS

Just as the Byzantine Empire kept alight the lamp of learning and civilisation in the Dark Ages so did it continue the traditions of Rome and Greece in its coinage. Its old traditions of coinage served as a model for the European states which emerged in the eighth and ninth centuries. The Byzantines minted coins in the three main metals, though their silver coins are comparatively scarce and usually debased by a high copper content. Justinian I was the first emperor to add a date to his coins, in the form of the year from the beginning of his reign in 526. Coins were produced on a flat disc flan up till the eleventh century when a curious concave shape was adopted for all denominations except the smallest bronze pieces. Such coins are known to collectors as *nummi scyphati* (saucer-shaped coins). The figure of Christ first appears on Byzantine coins about AD 450 and from the ninth century onwards many saints of the Orthodox Church – Theodore, George, Michael and John among others – were also portrayed. As time went on Greek replaced Latin in the inscriptions on these coins, and it is interesting to note how the Greek letters gradually took over from their Roman counterparts.

The coins of Byzantium had a tremendous influence on neighbouring territories. The medieval gold 'bezant' circulated widely throughout Europe and the Near East and was copied to a greater or lesser degree by the Caliphs of Baghdad and the Kings of Mercia.

Crude copies of late Roman coins were produced by the Ostrogoths from the end of the fifth century. Theodoric not only paid homage to the memory of Imperial Rome but slavishly imitated the gold coins of his Byzantine contemporary Anastasius, even going so far as to copy his titles and other inscriptions. The high regard in which the Byzantine gold coins was held is not unlike the reverence shown by the Arab world in recent times for the English gold sovereign and the Maria Theresa thalers which, dated 1782, have continued to be minted in various places right up to the present day!

Theodoric's successors, Athalaric and Theodahad, continued to imitate Roman and Byzantine coins, substituting their own portraits. For a time the Byzantine rulers succeeded in recapturing the Balkans and Italy and struck coins at the mints of Rome and Ravenna in the eighth and ninth centuries. Elsewhere in the Dark Ages gold and silver coins on Roman models were struck by the Vandals in North Africa, the Suevians in Spain, the Lombards in Italy, the Burgundians in northern France, the Visigoths in southern France, the Merovingians in central France and the Anglo-Saxons in England. In the majority of cases the coins followed Roman precedents, with crude portraits of local rulers and a wide variety of local inscriptions. In this period the right to strike coins extended to numerous towns and even monasteries. There were, for example, more than 800 different mints in the Merovingian Kingdom in the sixth and seventh centuries. The Merovingians introduced a new coin, the silver 'saiga', which was based on the Roman denarius and was

Byzantine bronze coin showing the portrait of Christ

Byzantium: Theophilus gold solidus (839–842 A.D.)

Byzantium: Justinian II gold solidus (685–717 A.D.)

Byzantium: Justinian II bronze 40 nummia (565–66 A.D.)

Arab-Byzantine bronze 40 nummia late 7th century

Examples of 12th century money
from the Chapter of St. Georges
de Bocherville in Normandy,
and monies of Henri I

France: Louis XIV obverse
and reverse, 1694

Vatican obverse and
reverse 20 centesimi 1931

the forerunner of the medieval 'denier' or 'penny', introduced by Pepin the Short in 755.

Under the Carolingian rulers gold coinage disappeared and the silver penny was the most popular unit of currency. The best-known coins in this period were minted by the Abbey of St Martin at Tours. The 'tournois' enjoyed wide circulation and survived in the words turner or tourney, meaning a small copper coin. Louis IX (1226–70) introduced the 'gros', a small silver coin which spread eventually across Europe in many different forms – 'grote', 'groat', 'groschen', 'groszy', 'grush' and even the Turkish 'kurus'.

Italy disintegrated during the middle ages into a multitude of petty principalities and city states. It was the cross-roads of different civilisations and came under the influence of Romans, Byzantines, Goths, Franks and Arabs. As a result the coinage of medieval Italy was extremely complicated and many different types of coin evolved. Pope Adrian I (772–95) minted the first papal coins, and these have continued in an unbroken line down to the present day. Many of these coins copied Roman models and, indeed, for a time they were struck in the name of the Senate and People of Rome. Many papal coins were engraved by the finest sculptors and medallists of the Renaissance and the beautiful 'ducats' and 'sequins' of the

Middle Ages have great historical significance, recording the upheavals of Italy in the struggles between Pope and Emperor.

The sequin, or 'zecchino', originated in Venice. The rival city of Florence produced a large silver coin in 1189, depicting a lily and St John the Baptist. This was the 'florin' which eventually passed into the currency of many countries and survives to this day in the Netherlands where the written abbreviation for a guilder is 'fl'. Handsome gold and silver coins were also struck at Genoa, Milan and Naples.

The medieval coinage of Germany was even more complex. The Frankish rulers were at first content to imitate the Romans and Byzantines, then the deniers or denars of the Carolingian monarchs. In the fourteenth century Louis of Bavaria introduced the 'grossus', modelled on the French gros. Earlier in that century a silver coin known as the 'bracteate' was adopted in many parts of Germany. It was so thin that it could be struck on one side only, thus creating an effect like the curious double-image coins of Magna Graecia mentioned in Chapter 2. The popularity of the bracteate is unaccountable, since these thin coins were very easily damaged, but examples were minted all over the German territory, from Prussia in the east to Franconia and Swabia. Gold coins were re-introduced in Germany, as in other parts of Europe, from the middle of the thirteenth century onwards, as the general level of prosperity recovered after the Dark Ages. Germany was technically welded together into the Holy Roman Empire (which also included much of Switzerland, Austria, Hungary, modern Czechoslovakia and parts of Italy). In practice however, it consisted of hundreds of tiny principalities, duchies, free cities and petty states, each of which had the right to issue its own coins. By the sixteenth and seventeenth centuries the currency of the Empire had become chaotic. Some of the biggest headaches confronting Switzerland and Germany when these countries emerged as unified nations in the nineteenth century was the confusion of currency systems.

Elsewhere in Europe the coinage followed existing patterns. In Spain and Portugal the coinage was closely modelled on the Arab dinar. In Belgium the coinage copied the contemporary money of France and the Holy Roman Empire. In the Scandinavian countries silver pennies of Anglo-Saxon type and bracteates on the German model were widely used. In Russia the princes of Kiev imitated the Byzantines.

The medieval period in European coinage ends with the discovery of rich silver deposits at

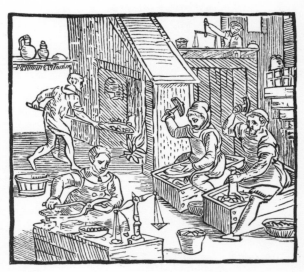

Far Left 13th century Exchequer tallies. **Left** Officers receiving and weighing coins at the Exchequer. AD 1130-1174. **Above** 16th century coiners at work

Joachimsthal in Bohemia. The Counts of Schlick, who mined the silver, struck large silver coins from 1518 onwards and these were nicknamed 'Joachimsthalers', soon shortened to thalers or talers. This large, handsome coin became popular all over Europe under many different guises – the 'daler' of Scandinavia to the 'talari' of Ethiopia, the 'tala' of Samoa and, of course, the 'dollar' which is now the universal unit of currency. In Spain this coin became the silver piece of eight 'reales' and, as such, enjoyed widespread usage in the Western Hemisphere where it is remembered by the broken eight in the dollar sign ($). The 'real' became known as a bit – hence the expression 'two-bit coin' for the American quarter dollar.

England adopted the thaler in 1551, but gave it a new name – the 'crown'. Elsewhere these large silver coins went under such names as 'corona', 'korun', 'krona', 'krone', 'kroon' and 'kruna' and though they have dwindled sadly in size these names have been retained as the unit of currency in many European countries to this day. In other countries the principal feature on this coin gave it its name. From the cross came the 'cruzeiro', still current in Brazil, while the heraldic shield, or escutcheon, adopted by Portugal and France became the 'escudo' and the 'ecu' respectively.

Because of its size the thaler, dollar or crown offered considerable scope to the coin engraver, at a time when interest in the medallic art was increasing. For this reason these coins are usually handsome and vigorously engraved and have a universal appeal to numismatists, many of whom specialise in dollar-sized coins.

Austria: thaler of 1703 showing Habsburg coat of arms

Spain: Ferdinand VII, 1823

Portugal: obverse and reverse of 400 reis coin of Don Pedro II, 1704

The design and engraving of money during the 16th century
Overleaf *'Grote Markt' at the Hague* by La Fargue
Inset *Adriana van Heusden and her daughter at the Fishmarket at Amsterdam* by De Witte

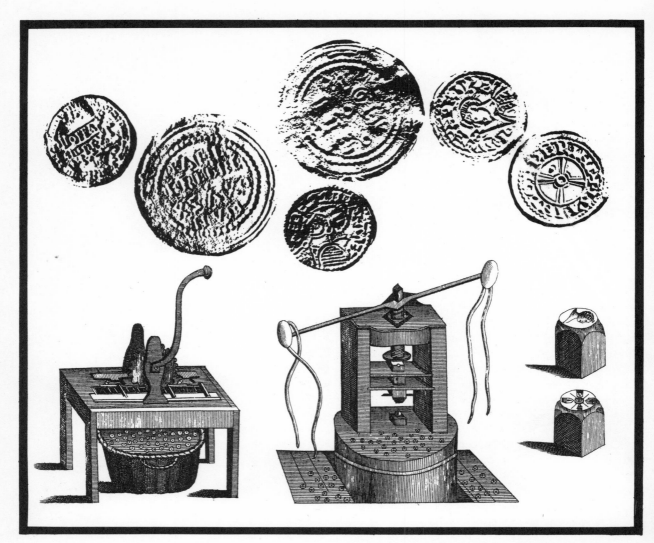

5 BRITISH COINS

Mediterranean traders sailed as far as the British Isles centuries before Christ in search of tin and iron ore. It seems likely that the first coins to circulate among the British tribes were the staters of ancient Greece. The Britons had a high regard for the gold 'philippeioi' minted by Philip of Macedon (359–336 BC) and, like the tribes across the Channel in Gaul, eventually struck their own crude imitations of these handsome coins. The portrait of Zeus and the charioteer on the reverse gradually disintegrated into a few meaningless squiggles, but the primitive imitations enjoyed wide currency in southern Britain. Traditionally Cunobelin, king of the Catovellauni of Hertford-shire in the first century BC, was the first ruler to strike coins bearing an inscription, though other minor kings, such as Tincommius, also minted crude coins.

The native British coinage came to an end after the Roman invasion and conquest in AD 43 and from then onward Roman imperial coins circulated in Britain. In AD 290, however, mints were set up at London and Colchester. The coins struck there closely followed the style of Roman coins, but they can be identified by their mint-marks and inscriptions. This was a period during which Carausius and Allectus broke away from the central authority of Rome and proclaimed an independent British Empire. Many of these coins depicted the female figure of Peace, reflecting a more friendly attitude towards Rome, and gradually the short-lived British Empire was brought under central control again.

Anglo-Saxon Coins

After the departure of the Roman legions at the beginning of the fifth century the Romano-British continued to mint coins on Roman lines. They soon began to deteriorate in quality of design and precious metal content. Archaeologists have not so far been able to discover coins of the legendary King Arthur, though there have been several false claims in recent years. Nevertheless the crude denarii and barbarous antoniniani of the fifth—seventh centuries may well have been the coins used by Arthur and his successors.

The invasions of tribes from northern Europe, the Angles, Saxons and Jutes, and the later raids by the Vikings from Scandinavia resulted in almost six centuries of extremely unsettled conditions in Britian. Peace and stability were not restored till long after the Norman Conquest in 1066. Little is known for certain regarding the coinage of this period. By the middle of the seventh century the kingdom of Mercia was using small silver coins known as 'sceats', with a wide variety of inscriptions in Runic lettering. At the same time the kingdom of Northumbria used copper coins called 'stycas' and these bore the crude effigy of kings from Ecgfrith (670–85) onwards. Offa of Mercia (757–96) coined gold imitations of Arab dinars with his own name, but is best remembered for introducing the silver penny, modelled on the contemporary Carolingian coins, but with a broader flan.

The silver pennies of Offa bore a fine likeness of the king, with his name on the obverse and the moneyer's name on the reverse. The silver penny was later adopted by the other Anglo-Saxon kingdoms of Kent, East Anglia and Wessex and for several centuries was the only coin used in what is now England. Pennies were minted by the Archbishops of Canterbury and under royal

Sceat of Alfred the Great

Gold coin of Archbishop
Wigmund of York

authority in many towns. By the time of Aethelred II there were more than 70 mints in England and often the name of the mint was added to the inscription on the reverse.

The standard of portraiture in these coins dropped sharply after the death of Offa. Eventually a system of tiny punches was adopted to create a rough likeness of the king. Dots, dashes, curved lines and squiggles, applied with various punches, built up a crude portrait. Similarly the reverse design became stereotyped, invariably with a cross as its chief motif.

Norman Coins

The Norman Conquest made little difference to the coins of England, except in the greater variety of coin dies and the frequency with which they were changed in a bid to defeat the forger. The coins continued to be crudely punched out. The most interesting coins in this period are those produced by the various factions in the civil war between Stephen and Matilda in the middle of the twelfth century.

Plantagenet Coins

The first of the Plantagenet kings, Henry II (1154–89) stopped the practice of changing the coin dies at frequent intervals and, in fact, stuck to one type until 1180. From then until 1247 the short cross penny was minted and continued to bear Henry's name through the reigns of his three successors. To the monotony of this period was added the further deterioration in standards, until the penny degenerated into a crudely punched disc, with little semblance of design and ill-formed lettering.

In 1247 Henry III introduced the 'long cross penny', in which the arms of the cross extended to the rim of the coin. The object of this was to prevent dishonest individuals from clipping silver off the edges. Since there were no coins of smaller value pennies were often cut in half or quarters, and the cross was a useful guide to the division of the coin. Cutting up the coins in this way only added to the possibility of fraud and this practice was forbidden by Edward I (1277–1327) who issued halfpennies and farthings to get round this problem. He also introduced the groat or fourpenny piece, imitating the Continental gros or grossus. The pennies of Edward I showed the king on the obverse and had a long cross, with three pellets between the arms, on the reverse.

Silver penny of Edward the Confessor, 1065 (enlarged twice normal)

Silver penny of Harold, 1066 (enlarged twice normal)

Edward III gold noble

A forestaller in the pillory, 1497

This type remained more or less constant until the reign of Henry VII.

Edward III (1327–77) introduced the 'half-groat' and began minting gold coins. In 1344 a set of three coins was issued, the gold florin being equal to 24 silver pennies, while its half and quarter denominations were known as the 'leopard' and the 'helm', from the principal subjects depicted on them. This gold coinage was unsuccessful and disappeared soon afterwards, being replaced by the gold 'noble' of 120gr, minted in 1351. Incidentally the obverse of this coin, showing the king standing in a ship, is said to commemorate the naval victory at Sluys in 1346 during the Hundred Years War with France. The noble had a value equal to 33p or 85c in modern currency, and there were also half and quarter nobles. These gold coins were mainly intended as a method of handling bullion in convenient form and vast quantities of these coins were shipped across the Channel and used to pay mercenary troops and allies in the struggle for control of France. This was the period of the so-called Anglo-Gallic coinage, when English coin types were produced at French mints during the English occupation. The claims of the English kings to the throne of France are alluded to in the inscriptions and the inclusion of the French *fleur-de-lys* in the design.

Henry V gold angel

York and Lancaster Coins

The century from the overthrow of Richard II in 1399 to the defeat of Richard III in 1485 was marked by defeats in France and long civil wars at home. Inevitably the English economy suffered terribly and this is reflected in the coinage of the times. The coins minted by the Yorkist and Lancastrian factions are comparatively scarce, since most of them seem to have been smuggled out of the country and melted down abroad.

Edward IV raised the value of the noble and added a rose to the design, hence the name 'rose-noble' or 'ryal' given to this coin. A new coin introduced at this time and called an 'angel', after the Archangel Michael depicted on the obverse. The reverse showed the cross of Christ in front of the mast of a ship. Because of its religous flavour the angel was popular all over Europe and was believed by many to have certain magical qualities. It was used as a touch-piece, for good luck, and was the coin used by the monarch in touching for the king's evil, the skin disease

38

Money-changers, 15th century

known as scrofula. For this purpose angels were struck as late as the reign of King Charles I, and smaller imitations were produced by the later Stuarts including the Old and Young Pretenders who also claimed the divine right of healing this disease.

Tudor Coins

Henry VII (1485–1509) introduced the gold 'sovereign' of 240 pence and subsequently (1500) added the 'shilling' of 12 pence to the range of coins in circulation. Originally this coin was known as a 'testoon' and it did not adopt its more familiar name until the reign of Edward VI. The archaic name is preserved to this day in Scots Gaelic, where 'tasdan' is used for a shilling.

Henry VIII squandered the fortune amassed by his father and then debased the currency to finance his extravagant projects. He added a considerable amount of copper to the silver coinage. The base shilling, which he introduced in 1544, had a full-face portrait of him, and soon earned the nickname of 'Old Coppernose', when the silver wore off the high point of his features. He introduced the gold crown of five shillings, raised the value of the angel and replaced it by the George 'noble', so-called on account of its picture of St George and the Dragon. Henry cut down the number of mints in England and abolished the mints operated by the Archbishops of Canterbury and York and the Bishop of Durham.

Edward VI replaced the gold crown by the large silver coin of the same name, modelled on the thalers of Bohemia which were then becoming very popular on the Continent. In the reign of Mary (1553–8) the portrait of her husband, Philip II of Spain, appeared briefly on the shilling. Elizabeth continued the same range of coins as her father. Rising prosperity during her reign led to a vast improvement in the precious metal content of the coinage. Elizabeth added the silver 'sixpence' and 'threepence', and these largely replaced the twopence and groat, though they continued to be minted. Some half-hearted experiments with mill and screw machinery led to a short-lived improvement in the appearance of the coins, but the mintworkers were so violently opposed to any mechanisation of their labours that the authorities were forced to give up the idea and revert to the production of hand-hammered coins. Dates began to appear regularly on English coins for the first time.

Elizabeth I sixpence

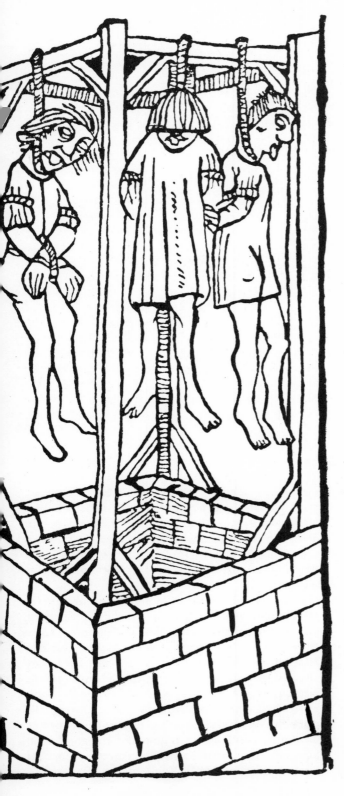

Hanging coin forgers
(from Villon's *Ballarde des Pendus)*

Stuart Coins

The accession of James VI of Scotland as King James I of England in 1603 inaugurated the most complicated period in the history of British coinage. To the existing range of coins James added the gold 'unite' (so-called since its design symbolised the union of the crowns of Scotland and England), the 'rose-ryal' and the 'spur-ryal', revived the angel and the half-angel, struck a variety of large silver coins known as the 'double-crown', the 'thistle crown' and the 'Britain crown', introduced the 'half-crown' and the 'laurel', 'half-laurel' and 'quarter-laurel'. At the other end of the scale he introduced the first copper coins minted in England since Anglo-Saxon times—the 'farthing'—but this was unpopular and soon disappeared from circulation.

Charles I continued many of these coin types, but the chief interest of his reign lies in the makeshifts produced by both sides in the Civil War. The Parliamentary forces soon gained control of the Royal Mint in London, but various provincial mints were established, at Aberystwyth, Oxford, York, Chester and Bristol among other places, and coins were struck there on behalf of the king. The Parliamentary Roundheads continued to strike coins bearing the king's effigy, right down till 1649 when he was beheaded. In addition silver plate was melted down and crude coins struck at Carlisle, Colchester, Newark, Pontefract and Scarborough while these towns were under siege. Hammered coins inscribed THE COMMONWEALTH OF ENGLAND were struck at London between 1649 and 1660.

One of the last acts of the Commonwealth was the re-introduction of mechanical equipment. The first milled coins (so-called because the screw was operated by a horse-mill or water-mill, and not on account of the grained edge) bore the profile of Oliver Cromwell 'warts and all', but had a very short life since he died shortly before they were issued. The first coins after the Restoration of Charles II were hammered but the mechanisation of the Royal Mint was completed in 1662 and from then onward all British coins were milled. 'Milling' is the popular, though incorrect, term for the grooves applied to the edge of coins. The proper term is graining and it was adopted to prevent people from clipping metal from the edge of coins. Actually the first security device took the form of an engraved inscription in Latin: *decus et*

Charles II guinea, 1663

James II guinea, 1687

tutamen – 'an ornament and a safeguard' thus leaving people in no doubt as to its purpose!

At the same time the previous confusion of coinage was drastically simplified. The multitude of gold coins was replaced by the 'guinea' of 21 shillings, with multiples of two and five guineas and the fractional half guinea. The coin took its name from the Guinea Coast of West Africa, whence much of the gold was acquired. The silver denominations, from the penny to the crown, continued as before. Charles also introduced the special series of little silver coins, in denominations of 1, 2, 3 and 4 pence, which he presented to the deserving poor during the annual Maundy Thursday ceremony. The coins are presented in leather purses to as many people of both sexes as the sovereign is years of age. The minting of these special silver coins has continued down to the present day.

The farthings of James I and Charles I had been struck by Lord Harrington under contract from the crown and were unpopular. The first attempt at a royal issue in base metal came in 1672 when copper halfpence and farthings were struck at the Royal Mint with the now famous Britannia reverse design.

The revolution of 1688 and the subsequent Williamite Wars in Ireland resulted in some curious makeshifts known as 'gun-money', since they were coined from gunmetal. The coins of William III and Mary are of interest since they showed the conjoined profiles – the portraits overlapping. After Mary's death in 1694 the coins bore the portrait of William alone. During the reign of Anne (1702–14) silver coins were minted with the word VIGO below the queen's neck, alluding to the treasure captured from the Spaniards by Sir George Rooke at Vigo Bay in 1702.

Obverse and reverse 6d. of
King George II

Hanoverian Coins

The value of the guinea fluctuated considerably during the wars at the turn of the eighteenth century but was finally fixed at 21 shillings in 1717. The coinage of the first three Georges was technically competent, though undistinguished in design. Coins were struck in gold ($\frac{1}{2}$ to 5 guineas) and in silver (sixpence to crown). Copper farthings were struck from time to time but half-pence and pennies in base metal were seldom produced, so that the shortage of small change had to be filled by 'tokens' struck by traders, inn-keepers and private individuals. The token coin-age of this period is discussed in greater detail in Chapter 11.

In 1745 Admiral Anson captured a Spanish treasure ship during his voyage round the world. Coins struck from the captured silver bore the word LIMA below the king's bust. Spanish dollars circulated in Britain at the end of the eighteenth century. They were countermarked with a tiny portrait of King George III or were crudely re-struck, with the king's profile and the effigy of Britannia more or less obliterating the original design.

The partnership of Matthew Boulton, the Birmingham manufacturer, and James Watt, the Scottish inventor of the steam engine, had wide repercussions on British coinage. Watt invented coining machinery powered by steam and this was eventually installed in a new Royal Mint, which moved from its original premises in the Tower of London in 1809. Some years earlier, however, Boulton and Watt were given the contract to mint copper coins in denominations of one penny and twopence and this resulted in the famous 'Cartwheels' of 1797. The Cartwheel two-pence weighed two ounces and was too heavy to become popular, though people found it useful as a weight. The scrap value of copper rose sharply soon afterwards, so the coins were withdrawn from circulation. In 1799 pennies and farthings were struck at the Soho Mint in Birmingham and continued to appear at irregular intervals till 1807 when base metal coins again disappeared from the scene.

The complete renewal of the Mint machinery was followed by a reform of the coinage, completed in 1816. The sizes and weights of the gold and silver coins were altered. The guinea of 21s was superseded by the 'sovereign' of 20s, though the same multiples and fraction (5 to $\frac{1}{2}$) were retained. Silver coins in denominations of three-pence, sixpence, one shilling, half-crown and crown were produced in the sizes and weights which remained in force until the introduction of decimal coinage in 1968–71. Copper coins were re-introduced in 1821. In 1860 the more durable bronze alloy was substituted and the size of the penny, halfpenny and farthing again reduced to the dimensions which they retained until the present reign.

Modern Coins

During the nineteenth century there were several experiments with other denominations. Apart from the tiny silver coins intended for the Maundy ceremony there were silver $1\frac{1}{2}$d and 4d (groats) which were circulated in certain British colonies where such denominations were necessary. The decimalisation of the coinage, eventually accomplished in 1971, was first proposed more than a century ago and led to the introduction of the

Halfpenny of George IV, 1827

Gothic florin, 1848 Queen Victoria

Obverse and reverse ½d. of
Queen Victoria 1855

Obverse and reverse of 6d.
of Queen Victoria

Halfpenny of Queen
Elizabeth

3d. of George V, 1919

Shilling of George V

3d. of George VI, 1938

Half-crown of George VI

'florin' in 1849, originally inscribed ONE TENTH OF A POUND. In the Queen Victoria Jubilee series of 1887 there was even a double-florin, worth four shillings. Nicknamed the 'Barmaid's Grief', it was unpopular since barmaids – and others – often mistook this coin for a crown and were therefore short-changed by a shilling.

Despite the increasing use of machinery in the production of coins, many of the coins of the nineteenth and twentieth centuries can be regarded as splendid examples of medallic art. The 'Gothic florin' (thus named on account of its Gothic lettering) and the standing 'Britannia florin' of Edward VII have long been popular with collectors on account of their attractive designs. The George and Dragon design of Benedetto Pistrucci was used on many sovereigns and crowns from 1816 up to the present day. British coins of the past 150 years have been fairly conservative in their subjects. Britannia graced the reverse of the bronze coins down to 1937 when the wren (farthing) and *Golden Hind* (halfpenny) were introduced. The royal coat of arms was the principal motif of the silver coins other than the crown. Numeral designs were adopted for the 3d and 6d in Edward VII's reign and the lion on crown design for the shilling at the same time. The lion on crown design was extended to the sixpence in the reign of George V and a new reverse, featuring the heraldic flowers of the United Kingdom, adopted for the threepence and sixpence in 1927.

The first major change in coin types came in 1937 when the George VI series was released. Apart from the bronze coins already mentioned the series was notable for two additions. A brass twelve-sided threepence depicting a clump of thrift was introduced, alongside the silver threepence which now showed the cross of St George superimposed on an English rose. The brass threepence, in a modified design with the profile of King Edward VIII, had also been prepared and a few examples accidentally got into circulation. As a mark of deference to the Scottish origins of the queen a Scottish shilling, with the lion rampant, was added to the set, while the English shilling continued the reverse design of the previous reign. The florin featured the crown and floral emblems, while the half-crown continued, in a modified form, the reverse design of the George V series. The last crowns minted for ordinary use appeared in 1934. Since then they have been struck for commemorative purposes and, as such, are dealt with in Chapter 10.

The silver content of British coins decreased in 1920, from 0·925 to 0·500, a fifty per cent nickel alloy being used instead. In 1947 the silver-nickel alloy was replaced by a copper-nickel alloy and from 1949 the inscription IND IMP (Emperor of India) was dropped from the design. No gold coins were struck for circulation after 1917, though they have been re-introduced in recent years for export to the Middle East, for use in bullion transactions and for sale to collectors.

The first series introduced by Queen Elizabeth II ranged from the bronze farthing to the cupro-nickel half-crown. The bronze denominations closely followed the Georgian designs, but new reverse types were adopted for the higher values. The brass threepence featured a portcullis gate, while floral emblems graced the sixpence and florin. There were two types of shilling, featuring the heraldic symbols of England and Scotland, and the royal coat of arms appeared on the half-crown. There was no silver threepence, the last of this type having been minted in 1941.

The humble farthing was last struck in 1956. The victim of rising inflation, this attractive little coin found little usage and ceased to be legal tender in 1960. The next victim of inflation and the change to decimal currency was the halfpenny, last minted in 1967. In 1968 the first decimal coins were introduced. The 5p (shilling) and 10p (florin) were struck in the same sizes as existing coins and featured the Scottish thistle and the royal lion respectively. The half-crown was withdrawn

from use at the end of 1968 and in February 1971 the penny and threepence were superseded by the new ½, 1 and 2 pence coins. The obsolete sixpence has won a temporary reprieve and still circulates as a 2½p coin, though it is likely to be phased out shortly. Another sign of the times was the re-introduction, in 1969, of a high denomination coin. This was the 50p (ten shillings), featuring Britannia on the reverse. This seven-sided coin, struck in cupro-nickel on a flan only slightly larger than the 10p coin, was greeted with howls of protest and the banks were forced to continue issuing obsolete ten-shilling notes for some time.

Other British Coins

This chapter has dealt mainly with the coinage of England, but it is important to remember that both Scotland and Ireland have also had distinctive coins at various times in their history, while the Channel Islands and the Isle of Man still have their own currency.

The earliest coins of Scotland were the silver pennies minted by David I from 1124 onwards. These coins were similar to the English coins of the time and differed only in their inscriptions. Scotland suffered inflation in the fourteenth and fifteenth centuries and by the time of King James I (1406—37) Scots money had sunk to a twelfth of its nominal value. This 12 to 1 ratio was maintained till the seventeenth century when Scottish coinage

Obverse florin of Queen Elizabeth

Britain: Queen Victoria farthing (old head)

Obverse half-crown of Queen Elizabeth

Britain: Queen Victoria (bun profile) farthing

Ireland: halfpenny of
George III, 1805

Irish Republic: florin, 1939

Irish Republic: shilling,
1939

Twelfth of a shilling Jersey

Obverse and reverse of 3d.
Guernsey

was discontinued. The majority of the coins were copper and featured the monarch on the obverse and the thistle on the reverse.

The first Irish coins were silver pennies minted by the Viking settlers in Dublin in the tenth century. After the Anglo-Norman invasion of Ireland in the twelfth century silver pennies were minted in the name of Prince John as Lord of Ireland. Later Irish coins closely followed English patterns. A rare 'half-farthing', bearing the name of St Patrick, was struck in the reign of Edward IV and a groat issued by Lambert Simnel as King Edward VI appeared at Dublin in 1487. The harp reverse design first appeared on Irish coins in the reign of Henry VIII and survived till the early nineteenth century when Irish coins were discontinued. The independence of the 26 counties resulted in a handsome series of coins, from farthing to half-crown, featuring a harp on the obverse and various birds, domestic animals and fish on the reverse. Coins from 1928 to 1938 were inscribed *Saorstat Eireann* (Irish Free State), while those from 1939 onwards have borne the simpler form *Eire* (Ireland).

The Channel Islands have been issuing their own coins, off and on for six centuries and, though many of them have conformed to British sizes and weights, have often produced unusual shapes and denominations. Coins of four and eight 'doubles', equivalent to the British halfpenny and penny, have been minted at various times, as well as sixpences with scalloped edges and a curious rectangular ten-shilling coin.

The first coins of the Isle of Man appeared in the eighteenth century and featured the three-legged emblem of the island. These coins continued until 1864. A series of gold coins was produced in 1967, a handsome silver crown depicting a tail-less Manx cat in 1970 and a regular series from ½ to 50p re-introduced in 1971. The Irish Republic, Guernsey and Jersey have also produced decimal sets in 1971 which parallel the British series.

No account of British coinage would be complete without some reference to the 'puffins' and 'half-puffins' of Lundy, in the Bristol Channel. These bronze coins, named after the island's commonest sea-bird, appeared in the 1930s as part of the scheme of the proprietor, Martin Coles Harman, to have himself recognised as King of Lundy. He was, however, prosecuted in the English courts and his coins withdrawn from circulation, though they remain popular with collectors to this day.

46

British decimal series,
1968-71 $\frac{1}{2}$, 1, 2, 5, 10
and 50 pence

The Stock Exchange, 1844

ENGLISH
GOLD COINS

Left: Henry VIII silver groat c. 1500
This Page Top: Henry III gold penny
Bottom: Henry VII sovereign

6 AMERICAN COINS

The Spaniards voyaged to the New World in search of precious metals and for almost three hundred years they exported vast quantities of gold and silver to Europe. The bulk of this was coined before it left America. Mints were set up at Lima, Potosi, Mexico and other cities in New Granada, as the Spanish territory was called, and there the famous 'pieces of eight' and gold 'doubloons' were struck. Every year the treasure fleets sailed from Latin America for Spain, laden with bullion and coin which made Spain the richest and most powerful nation in Europe, and eventually these coins found their way into every part of the world. The basic designs of these coins altered little over the years. The early pieces of eight had the Spanish coat of arms on one side and an elaborate cross motif on the other. In 1732 a

new design, showing the pillars of Hercules, was introduced. The gold 'escudo' of sixteen reales used similar designs. This minting of Spanish-American coinage continued till the early years of the nineteenth century when the Spanish colonies declared their independence.

During the period when Spanish coins were being minted in Central and South America, other European powers – the British, Dutch, Swedes, French and Danes – were developing North America. To a large extent the North American colonies and the West Indies used Spanish dollars and escudos as currency, but gradually minor coinage for purely local use began to appear. The Pilgrim Fathers and the other early settlers had little need of money, and carried on barter with the Indians, using such things as beads, tobacco and the like. A certain amount of British currency circulated in New England but no attempt was made by the mother country to provide for its colonies. In 1652 John Hull of Massachusetts Bay Colony struck crude shillings, sixpences and threepences. The plain circular flan was inscribed NE (New England) and the value in Roman numerals. Something more elaborate was called for, so coins depicting a willow or an oak-tree in the same denominations were struck later the same year. These coins also bore the name of the colony, rendered as MASATHVSETS. They had the date 1652 and this remained unchanged for more than thirty years. A series depicting a pine tree was minted between 1667 and 1682, though they also bore the date 1652. Twopences were struck in 1662.

Cecilius, Lord Baltimore struck coins in copper (penny) and silver (fourpence, sixpence and shilling) bearing his portrait or coat of arms. They circulated in Maryland from 1658 onwards. New Jersey's first coins were halfpence and farthings imported from Dublin in 1681–2 and showed a fine effigy of St Patrick. Token coinage was minted by William Wood between 1722 and 1733. Wood also struck the first coins intended for use throughout the American plantations. They depicted a crowned rose and were inscribed *Rosa Americana*, the name by which they are commonly known to collectors. Wood used an alloy known as Bath metal, containing silver, brass, copper and zinc. These 'plantation pieces', in denominations of halfpenny, penny and twopence, portrayed King George I on the obverse.

During the American War of Independence (1776–83) the rebel colonies used paper money to pay their troops. This 'Continental currency', as it was called, even bore inscriptions in the name of His Majesty King George III! Although the Continental Congress passed a resolution to establish a mint as early as 1777, it was not until 1792 that the United States mint was opened at Philadelphia and the first coins were dated 1793. In the interim, however, various essays or trial pieces were produced and these are now of the greatest rarity. Among these trial pieces were the 'Nova Constellatio' coins engraved by William Wyon and struck at the Soho Mint in Birmingham.

The first coins struck at Philadelphia were 'cents' and 'half-cents', both depicting the head of Liberty. The designs were changed the following year so the original versions are now very rare and expensive. Originally the half cent showed Liberty facing left, while the coins of 1794 on-

Obverse and reverse of the silver half dime

Obverse (Washington) and reverse (eagle) of quarter dollar

wards showed her facing right. The first cents depicted Liberty with wind-swept hair, whereas the 1794 version tidied her locks and included the cap of liberty on a pole. To complicate matters still further the 1793 cents were produced with two reverse designs, showing the value encircled by a chain or a wreath. Half cents disappeared from circulation in 1857 and the size of the cent was reduced to its present dimensions in the same year. The large cents all featured Liberty in various poses. The first small cents (1857–8) pictured an eagle in flight. In 1859 the first of the Indian head cents was released and this design remained in use till 1909 when replaced by a portrait of Abraham Lincoln. Until 1958 Lincoln cents had a reverse design showing the words of value in a wheat-spray, but since then the Lincoln Memorial in Washington has appeared on the reverse. During the Second World War cents were struck in zinc-coated steel instead of bronze.

A two-cent coin, in bronze, was issued between 1864 and 1873, while 3 cent coins were released between 1851 and 1889. The first of the 3 cent coins was struck in silver and showed a shield inside a star on the obverse. Subsequently 3 cent coins depicting Liberty were minted in nickel.

From 1794 to 1873 silver coins worth 5 cents bore the inscription 'Half Dime' and depicted either the head of Liberty or the seated figure of Liberty. In 1866 a larger coin, inscribed 5 cents and struck in nickel, was introduced and gradually superseded the half dime. This coin, popularly known as a 'nickel', has had four basic designs in over a century. The first type had a shield obverse and the value (5) on the reverse. From 1883 to 1912 the obverse showed a head of Liberty and the value appeared as a Roman numeral (V) on the reverse. The nickels of 1913–38 showed an Indian and a buffalo respectively, and those issued since 1938 have portrayed Thomas Jefferson and his home at Monticello.

'Dimes', as the 10 cent coins are known, have been struck since 1796 and have varied considerably in design over the years. The first dimes featured a standing eagle on the obverse but from 1798 to 1807 was replaced by a heraldic eagle. No dimes appeared in 1808, but those from 1809 to 1837 showed Liberty wearing a cap. From 1837 to 1891 a seated Liberty appeared on the coins. For the coins of 1892 to 1916 Liberty faced left, while those from 1916 to 1945 showed her facing right. Since 1946 a profile of Franklin D. Roosevelt has appeared on the dime. Dimes were struck in

Reverse (Lincoln memorial) of the bronze 1c 1970

USA Liberty head dime, 1907

USA Indian head cent, 1899

USA 2 cents, 1864

USA 3 cents nickel 1867

Obverse (liberty) and reverse (V) of the first nickel 5c

Nickel 5c (Monticello building (reverse) Thomas Jefferson (obverse)

silver until 1964, and in nickel since that date.

Twenty-cent coins made a brief appearance, from 1875 till 1878, with a seated Liberty obverse and an eagle reverse. The quarter dollar (two bits or 25 cents) appeared in 1796, with a Liberty obverse and an eagle reverse. No coins of this denomination were minted again until 1804–7, when a heraldic eagle was depicted. There were no further quarter dollars till 1815 when coins in a reduced size were introduced. All quarters since that date have featured the eagle on the reverse, though the obverse designs have varied considerably – capped head of Liberty (1815–38), seated Liberty (1838–91), wreathed head of Liberty (1892–1916) and a standing figure of Liberty (1916–30). Since 1932 quarters have portrayed George Washington. Nickel has been used instead of silver since 1964.

The half dollar (50 cents) is the most varied of all American coins in regular use. Those minted between 1794 and 1840 were struck on a large flan, but the size has been standardised since then. Liberty with flowing hair (1794–5), draped bust (1796–1807), capped Liberty (1807–39), seated Liberty (1839–91), Liberty head (1892–1915), walking Liberty (1916–47) graced the obverse of these coins, while the eagle appeared on the reverse. In 1947 a new type, with Benjamin Franklin on the obverse and the Liberty Bell in Philadelphia on the reverse, was introduced. Normally this coin would have been current for 25 years, but as a mark of respect for President Kennedy, assassinated in 1963, his profile was placed on the obverse in 1964 and a heraldic eagle reverse was re-introduced. The first Kennedy half dollars were minted in 0·900 fine silver, but subsequent dates have been produced in 0·400 fine silver.

Silver dollars, with Liberty obverse and eagle reverse, were minted in 1794–1804 and then from 1840 till 1935, the various styles being parallel to the designs of the lower denominations. The last dollars, from 1921 to 1935 showed the head of Liberty emitting sun-rays. The United States also produced a trade dollar, from 1878 to 1889, inscribed with the weight and fineness of the silver – 420 grains 0·900 fine.

Coins struck at the Philadelphia mint do not bear a mint-mark. In certain years, however, various coins were minted elsewhere and such coins bear a letter indicating the mint, either D (Denver) or S (San Francisco). No mint-mark has appeared on coins struck since 1965.

Gold coins have also been minted at various

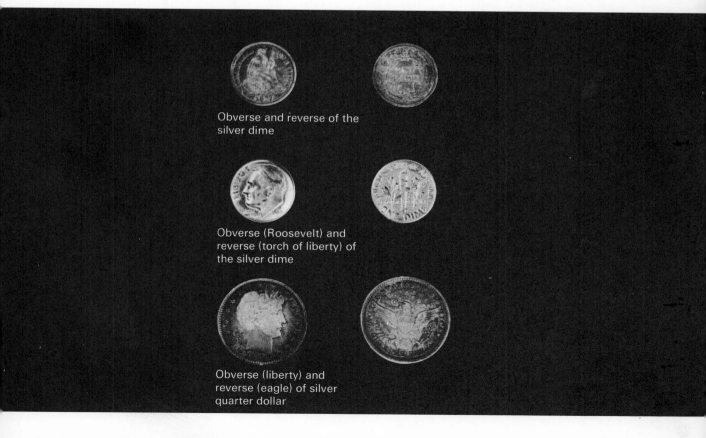

Obverse and reverse of the silver dime

Obverse (Roosevelt) and reverse (torch of liberty) of the silver dime

Obverse (liberty) and reverse (eagle) of silver quarter dollar

times. The 'eagle', or ten-dollar piece, was minted at intervals between 1795 and 1804 and again from 1838 to 1907. Half and quarter eagles were minted from time to time, and other denominations, of $1, $2, $3, $4, $20 and $50, have been produced, though mainly for commemorative purposes.

Commemorative silver coins, consisting mainly of half dollars, but occasionally quarters or dollars, have been minted since 1892 and are discussed in Chapter 10.

Latin America

Mexico City had a mint as early as 1536 and coined Spanish currency down till 1811. During the war of independence temporary mints operated at San Felipe de Chihuahua and Durango and royalist coins were often countermarked by the rebels. The silver coins minted since independence feature the Mexican eagle and the dollar-sized 'pesos' were popular as trade coins all over the world because of their high silver content. During the Civil Wars of 1913–20 temporary issues were produced by the various factions including the armies of Pancho Villa and Emiliano Zapata. The present series of 'centavos' and pesos is struck in brass, bronze and cupro-nickel, with occasional commemorative pieces in silver.

Farther south, the five republics of Central America – Costa Rica, Honduras, Guatemala, Nicaragua and Salvador – originally issued coins of a common type showing the five mountain peaks of the Isthmanian Federation. Though the federation disintegrated in the mid-nineteenth century the five peaks motif has been retained on many of the coins of these countries. The coinage of South America is extensive and space does not permit any detailed account. Of principal interest to collectors are the various dollar-sized coins such as the 'boliviano' of Bolivia, the 'balboa' of Panama, the 'sol' of Peru, the 'sucre' of Ecuador and the 'peso' of Argentina or Columbia. Brazil used a currency based on the Portuguese 'reis' and its dollar equivalent was the 'milreis', now superseded by the 'cruzeiro'. Apart from the large silver coins the lesser denominations, particularly those of the present day, offer tremendous scope and variety in the different metals used. In Argentina nickel-clad steel is used, Brazil employs stainless steel, cupro-nickel or pure nickel for its coins, the current Colombian series ranges from the copper-plated iron 'centavo' to the nickel-clad steel 50c and the cupro-nickel 5 pesos, a clad-metal 'sandwich' is used for Panamanian coins, while Uruguay now uses nickel-brass. Coats of arms, allegorical figures and portraits of statesmen form the bulk of the subjects depicted on the coins of Latin America.

USA Kennedy half dollar

USA gold eagles ($20 pieces)

Mexico 5 centavos: eagle
and serpent

Mexico 20 centavos, 1944

Mexico 5 pesos: eagle
and serpent

Coin minted at Caracas
(Venezuela) 1818

Panama silver balboa

Venezuela gold coin of
1887

Venezuela silver
venezolano 1930

7
BRITISH
COMMONWEALTH
COINS

Although this is now a vast field, the coinage of
the British Commonwealth is comparatively
modern. With the exception of the Indian subcontinent, whose coins extend in an unbroken
line from the Hellenistic issues of Bactria and the
curious lead coins of the Ardhras in the third
century BC, to the gold 'mohurs' of the Mogul
emperors and the 'rupees' of the present day,
Commonwealth coinage dates no farther back
than the early seventeenth century. The earliest
colonial coins were the 'hogge' money of Bermuda,
so-called because they depicted wild pigs on the
obverse. These coins were struck in copper with
a silver wash and were used from 1616 onwards.
Coinage soon spread to the British colonies on the
America mainland but, as forerunners of United
States money, these coins are dealt with in the
previous chapter.

Canada

As in other parts of the American continent,
Canada originally made do with Spanish pieces of

Canada large cent, King
George V, 1911

Canada 5 cents, 1950

Prince Edward Island
cent, 1871

Canada 1 cent, 1961

eight. Barter of animal skins and dried fish gave way to a system of token coinage (see Chapter 11) and this in turn was superseded by the issue of proper coins in the Confederation of Canada in 1870. At first token cents were struck in bronze and continued to circulate freely, but silver 5, 10, 25 and 50 cent pieces were introduced in that year. Large bronze cents were issued in 1876, though British halfpence continued to circulate for several years thereafter. The Victorian coins of Canada portrayed the queen on the obverse and the date and value in a wreath on the reverse. Similar cents, with distinctive inscriptions, were used in Prince Edward Island, Novia Scotia and New Brunswick till 1900, while Newfoundland (which did not join the Confederation till 1949) issued its own coins till that date.

The same basic types continued till 1920 when the size of the cent was greatly reduced and the maple leaf reverse was introduced. The silver 5 cent coin was replaced by a somewhat larger nickel coin in 1921. The first silver dollar appeared in 1935 to celebrate the Silver Jubilee of King George V. Since then silver dollars have been minted at various times for commemorative purposes.

The George VI series of Canada adopted a more pictorial appearance, with a schooner on the 10c, caribou moose on the 25c and the coat of arms on the 50c. During the Second World War the 5c coin underwent a number of changes, being struck in tombac brass and then in steel, during a shortage of nickel. A new design, featuring the 'V' for Victory symbol, temporarily replaced the beaver on the 5c coins. It is not always realised that the beaded border of these coins is, in fact, Morse code for 'We win when we work willingly'. The 5c coin also changed from a circular to a twelve-sided flan, like the contemporary British threepences. The same basic designs were retained for the Queen Elizabeth II series of 1953. Gold sovereigns circulated in Canada and were even struck at the Ottawa Mint on several occasions with the mint-mark C for Canada on the ground beneath the horse. In addition gold 5 and 10-dollar pieces were struck from 1912 to 1914.

Australia shilling reverse:
coat of arms 1947

Australia shilling reverse:
merino ram

Australia Captain Cook
50c, 1970

Australia polygonal 50c,
1969

Australia

Like Canada, Australia used Spanish dollars and barter long before introducing its own coinage. In the early nineteenth century a wide range of different currencies was used in Australia, including British, Portuguese, Dutch and Indian gold, silver and bronze coins. The chronic shortage of small change led to the issue of 'holey' dollars in 1813. Spanish dollars had their centres punched out. The centre 'plug' was equivalent to one shilling and threepence, while the outer ring did service as five shillings. The small circular part was known as a dump, and had the words 'Fifteen Pence' stamped across it. The holey dollar was stamped with its new value on one side and the words NEW SOUTH WALES and the date on the other. The value of dumps and holey dollars declined gradually to 1s 1d and 3s 9d respectively and by 1829 they were taken out of circulation.

Subsequently token coins were produced by private individuals and many of these circulated as late as 1868. Following the discovery of gold in Australia in 1851 gold dust, and later gold bars and ingots, served as currency. In 1853 a branch of the Royal Mint was opened in Sydney and subsequently branches were established in Melbourne (1872) and Perth (1899) with the object of converting gold into sovereigns. The Australian ones, like the Canadian sovereigns, bore mint-marks—

Australia 20 cents reverse:
platypus

Australia florin, 1947

Australia shilling, 1922

S, M or P. British silver and bronze coins circulated well into the present century. The first true Australian coins were minted in 1910 but were short-lived because of the death of King Edward VII. During the early years of George V's reign coins in bronze and silver were struck for Australia at the mints in London and Calcutta. The Australian mints took over responsibility for striking their own coins in 1918. The bronze half-pennies and pennies bore the value in words on the reverse while the silver coins featured the Australian coat of arms. Australia never minted half-crowns, though crowns appeared in 1937–8. The series of George VI was more pictorial, with a kangaroo on the bronze coins, ears of wheat on the 3d, the coat of arms on the 6d and florin and a merino ram on the shilling. The same types continued in the Elizabethan sterling set, but entirely new designs were adopted in 1966 for a series from 1 to 50 cents. Some of Australia's exotic wildlife appeared on the lower values while the coat of arms was retained on the 50c. Australia has also produced a number of interesting commemorative coins since 1927.

New Zealand

New Zealand has often been called the Britain of the South Pacific for its close identification with the British way of life. In numismatics this is particularly true. British coins were legal tender in New Zealand until recently and no attempt was made to issue distinctive coins until 1933 when the value of the New Zealand pound in relation to sterling fell and it became worthwhile to smuggle coins out of the country. This caused a shortage of coins in circulation and had to be remedied by the introduction of silver threepence, sixpence, shilling, florin and half-crown denominations. Bronze halfpennies and pennies did not appear till 1940. All New Zealand coins down to the present day are struck at the Royal Mint.

Curiously enough the Maori, who settled in New Zealand long before the coming of the white man, had no use for gold, but prized greenstone and fashioned it into tikis and other forms of personal adornment. Appropriately the tiki was featured on the bronze halfpenny. The subjects of the other coins were a tui on a kowhai branch (1d), crossed patu or clubs (3d), huia bird (6d), Maori warrior (1s), kiwi (2s) and coat of arms (2s 6d). Decimal currency was introduced in July 1967 and the subjects depicted are fern-leaf (1c), kowhai flowers (2c), tuatara lizard (5c), Maori carved head (10c), kiwi (20c) and Captain Cook's ship *Endeavour* (50c). New Zealand has issued commemorative coins since 1935 when a crown celebrated the Silver Jubilee of King George V.

Australia threepence, 1955

Australia penny, 1964

New Zealand sixpence, 1965

Australia 10 cents, 1968

New Zealand penny, 1946

New Zealand half-crown,
1949

New Zealand halfpenny,
1964

New Zealand florin reverse:
kiwi 1964

South Africa penny, 1949

South Africa large cent,
1961

Africa

For the sake of convenience the Republic of South Africa is usually grouped with the British Commonwealth. Prior to the union in 1910 the separate provinces issued their own coins. The earliest issues of the Cape of Good Hope were the 'rixdalers' produced by the Dutch East India Company in the seventeenth century. These and the 'veld-ponds' (field pounds) produced during the Boer War of 1899–1902 are rare and very expensive to buy nowadays, but there is plenty of scope for the collector of more modest means in the coins of the present century. The founding of the first Dutch settlement in 1652 by Jan van Riebeeck is alluded to time and time again in the coins of South Africa. His ship *Dromedaarius* appeared on the reverse of coins, from the ordinary penny to the commemorative crown of 1952, while his portrait graces the obverse of the present series of cents. Other subjects have included the covered wagons of the Voortrekkers, birds, animals and flowers. The first of the decimal coins included ½ and 1c coins in a brass alloy on the same large flans as the former halfpenny and penny, but since 1965 these denominations have been filled by small bronze coins.

Southern Rhodesia began issuing its own coins in 1932. Before that British and South African coins circulated. The wildlife of the country formed the subjects of the original series. A series for the Central African Federation of Rhodesia and Nyasaland appeared in 1955. Individual sets have been released by Rhodesia (Southern Rhodesia), Malawi (Nyasaland) and Zambia (Northern Rhodesia). Fauna and flora have provided the subjects for these coins. Decimalisation, rather than political upheavals, has influenced the coinage of these countries in recent years. Rhodesia's coins were inscribed in both pence and cents during the changeover, while both Malawi and Zambia have adopted the 'kwacha' divided into 100 'tambala' or 100 'ngwee' respectively.

The four British territories of the Gambia, the Gold Coast, Nigeria and Sierra Leone were grouped together in 1911 and coins inscribed British West Africa put into circulation. A curious feature of this coinage was the use of nickel for the lowest denominations – penny, halfpenny and one tenth of a penny. Nigeria had a limited issue of its own in 1907 and since 1957 has again issued its own coins. With the granting of independence separate issues of coins have been made by Ghana (the former Gold Coast), Sierra Leone and the Gambia. Both Mauritius and the

South Africa 20 cents,
1965

South Africa obverse of
1965 series: Van Riebeeck

Southern Rhodesia penny,
1941

South Africa reverse of 6d.
1953

South Africa 5 cents, 1965

South Africa reverse of 3d.
1951

Rhodesia and Nyasaland
penny, 1963

Zambia sixpence, 1964
obverse and reverse

Southern Rhodesian
reverse of half-crown,
1954

Zambia shilling, 1964

Rhodesia reverse of
shilling: coat of arms

Rhodesia reverse of florin:
secretary bird

Malawi half-crown reverse:
coat of arms

Rhodesia reverse of half-
crown: antelope

Malawi florin reverse:
elephants

Zambia crown obverse:
Dr. Kaunda, reverse: arms

Zambia obverse of 1964
series

Sierra Leone penny 1791

Seychelles now issue their own coins, replacing the Indian rupees which used to circulate there.

The earliest coins used in East Africa were the handsome 'hellers' and rupees of German East Africa (Tanganyika). Indian currency, British coins and cowrie shells were superseded by a general series of British East Africa which circulated in Kenya, Uganda and Tanganyika. To this day the East African Community continues its policy of a common currency, although commemorative pieces have been issued in the component countries.

West Indies

British coins circulated widely in the British West Indies, and, in fact, the pennies minted in 1950–1 were produced exclusively for use in these islands though a few eventually found their way back to the United Kingdom. Jamaica introduced a series of coins, from farthing to three halfpence in 1880. These coins, struck in cupro-nickel, were among the first coins in this alloy anywhere in the world. In more recent times United States currency largely superseded British coins in circulation. In the 1950s sets of coins in British Carribbean cents and dollars were introduced. Many of the individual colonies have also issued commemorative coins, such as the Commonwealth Games crown of Jamaica in 1966. Distinctive sets of coins have been issued in British Honduras and British Guiana. The Bahamas introduced a series of gold coins in denominations of $10, $20, $50 and $100 in 1968. In 1969 Jamaica abandoned sterling and introduced a decimal currency with bronze 1c and cupro-nickel 5, 10, 20 and 25c. The coat of arms appeared on the obverse, while the reverse designs featured flowers, a crocodile and the doctor bird, Jamaica's national emblem.

The Pacific Islands

For all practical purposes British, and latterly Australian or New Zealand, coins circulate in the various British colonies and protectorates of the Pacific. Fiji introduced a series of low denomination coins in 1934 with reverse subjects showing a sailing vessel, turtle and native hut. The same basic designs have been retained down to the present time. Tonga hit the headlines in numismatic circles in 1963 by issuing a series of three gold coins in denominations of quarter, half and one 'koula' (the Polynesian word for gold). This was hailed as the first gold coinage of Polynesia,

Nigeria shilling, 1959

East Africa shilling, 1952

Seychelles rupee, 1969

British Honduras 25 cents, 1962

Fiji penny, 1959

but it is unlikely that any of these attractive coins, portraying Queen Salote, actually got into circulation. In 1967 a series of commemorative coins marked the coronation of King George Tupou IV and included a coin, the 'hau', struck in palladium (a rare metal of the platinum group). This coin was equivalent to £40 sterling, weighed 1,000 Imperial grains and was 1¾ inches in diameter, thus making it the largest, heaviest and most valuable coin produced since the end of the eighteenth century. Needless to say, the average Tongan was unlikely to see any of these coins in his lifetime! Commemorative coins have subsequently appeared in the Cook Islands and Samoa.

Europe

Like India, Malta had a long numismatic history before the British acquired the island at the beginning of the nineteenth century. The earliest coins attributed to the island were struck by Phoenician traders in the third century BC. Subsequently there was a limited, and very rare, coinage under Greek and Roman influence. The Knights of St John occupied Malta from 1530 till

Sheep watering at a well in South Africa

1798 when they were ousted by Napoleon, and coins, in denominations from the diminutive 'picciolo' (72 equalled one penny) to the 'zecchino' (third of a pound sterling), were minted by authority of successive Grand Masters from De L'Isle Adam (1533) to Hompesch (1798). The French garrison, blockaded by the British, produced siege coins in gold, silver and bronze, in 1799–1800. Ordinary British coins have circulated since that date.

Gibraltar, captured by the British in 1704, used British and Spanish currency, though small denomination copper coins, of half, one and two quarts, appeared in 1842. Cupro-nickel crowns featuring the triple-towered emblem of Gibraltar were introduced in 1968. Cyprus has had its own coinage since 1879, following the acquisition of the island by the British from the Turks. The early coins featured the Crusader's coat of arms, an allusion to Richard the Lionheart who ruled Cyprus in the 12th century. A new series was introduced in 1955 when the pound of 1000 mils was adopted. Coins up to 100 mils were issued and featured animals and ships. A series of republican coins was put into circulation in 1963. The Ionian Islands, occupied by Britain from 1814 till 1864 when they were ceded to Greece, had a series of 'obol' denominations from 1819 onwards, featuring the lion of St Mark on the obverse and Britannia on the reverse. Incidentally, the half, third and quarter farthings minted by Britain at various times from 1827 to 1913 were intended mainly for circulation in these European territories.

Asia

India has a long numismatic history which is more appropriately dealt with in Chapter 9. The

An Australian aborigine

Cyprus 100 mils, 1955

earliest European coinage for India was produced by the Portuguese in the late sixteenth century. Later the Dutch, Danes and French minted coins for use in their own trading settlements in India. The East India Company issued coins of varying denominations in different parts of the subcontinent under its control. By 1835 a standardised coinage was introduced for the whole of British India. Coins in denominations of 'pies', 'pice', 'annas' and 'rupees' were struck by the Company and subsequently by authority of the British government which took over control of India in 1857. The coins of British India bore the profile of the ruler on the obverse and the value in words on the reverse. This practice continued up to the emergence of the dominions of India and Pakistan in 1947. India has been fond of unusual shapes, other than the orthodox circle. Rectangles and scalloped circles have been popular. The modern currency of both India and Pakistan is based on the rupee of 100 *paise*, and features the Asokan column and the Islamic toughra respectively.

The mandated territory of Palestine issued its own coins from 1927 till 1948 when the independent state of Israel emerged. The coins of the mandatory period were inscribed in English,

Palestine 20 mils

India silver rupee, 1901

India rupee obverse:
Nehru 1964

India one anna scalloped
edge, 1929

India "square" 2 annas,
1943

Arabic and Hebrew and ranged from the small bronze 1 'mil' featuring an olive branch to the large cupro-nickel coins with a hole in the centre.

The Straits Settlements issued coins, from the days of the East India Company onwards, and was the forerunner of the series of Malaya and British Borneo, with numeral designs, current in the 1950s, and the present series of Malaysia featuring the government buildings in Kuala Lumpur. Singapore also issues its own coins, in denominations from 10c to a dollar. Hong Kong issues coins in brass or cupro-nickel, with Chinese and English inscriptions on the reverse.

Ceylon has, like India, a coinage going back for many centuries. First the Portuguese (early sixteenth century), then the Dutch (1658) issued 'tangas'. In 1784 the Dutch coined silver rupees with inscriptions in Malay Arabic. Following the British occupation of the island in 1795 the existing system of 'rixdollars' and 'stuivers' was continued but the coins featured an elephant on the reverse and a portrait of King George III on the obverse. British half and quarter farthings and three halfpence silver coins circulated in Ceylon in the nineteenth century. The rupee of 100 cents was adopted in 1872 and a series of coins with a palm-tree motif was issued.

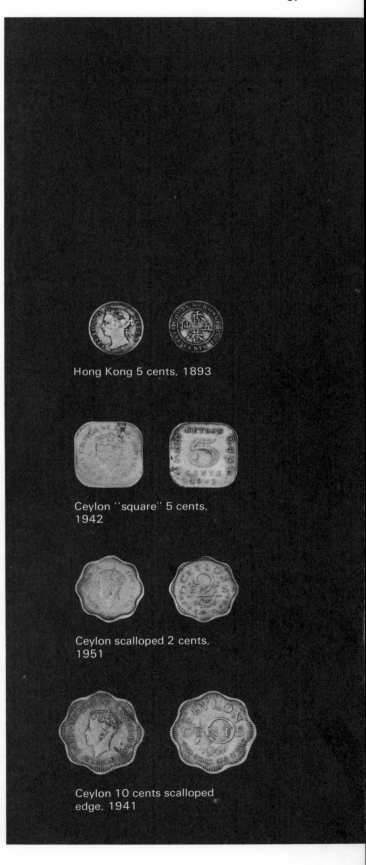

Hong Kong 5 cents, 1893

Ceylon "square" 5 cents, 1942

Ceylon scalloped 2 cents, 1951

Ceylon 10 cents scalloped edge, 1941

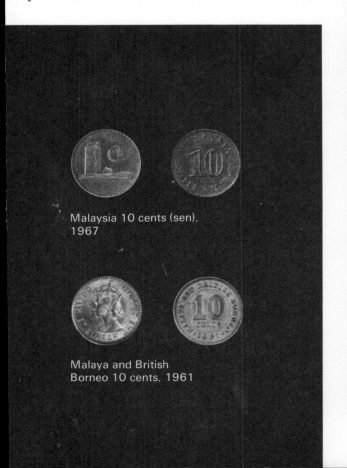

Malaysia 10 cents (sen), 1967

Malaya and British Borneo 10 cents, 1961

8
MODERN
EUROPEAN
COINS

It would be impossible to do more than outline the scope of this vast field. In the majority of cases the countries of Europe can boast a numismatic history going back many centuries and many collectors would prefer to concentrate on the coins of one country alone. The great trading nations, like Portugal and Spain, had a fairly conservative policy regarding their coins. Just as the owls of Athens remained virtually unchanged for centuries, so also the 'eight-real' coins and 'escudos' of the Iberian countries tended to remain fairly constant. Their universal popularity demanded that they should change as little as possible to keep faith with their customers.

At the other end of the scale the coins of the German states form a very large and complicated group, especially if the coinage of Austria, Bohemia and Switzerland is included. 'Thalers', 'doppeldicken', 'batzen', 'rappen', 'hellers', 'kronen', 'silbergroschen', 'gutegroschen', 'gulden', 'schillings' and 'marks'—these are only a few of the many different types of coin which the collector may come across. Every small state produced its own coins and the exchange rates with the currency of neighbouring states was usually very complicated. The coins of the eighteenth and nineteenth centuries are still reasonably plentiful, though such is the demand for them nowadays that they have increased greatly in price in recent years. On the other hand the coins of the twentieth century offer considerable scope at a smallish outlay. The major countries of Europe are discussed below, in alphabetical order.

Austria

The small silver coins of the late Middle Ages, the so-called 'Wiener Pfennige' (Vienna Pennies), bearing portraits of the dukes of Austria and kings of Bohemia, are expensive if they are in fine condition. The thalers, minted from the early sixteenth century onwards, also include many expensive items. The most famous of these, the 'Maria Theresa' thaler of 1782, is very common since it has been struck at several mints down to the present day for circulation in the Middle East. Austria continues to strike gold ducats and these are available to collectors. The ordinary coinage of Austria has undergone many changes in the past century. The florin or gulden consisted of 60 kreuzer, but the currency was decimalised in 1858 to the gulden of 100 kreuzer and this was superseded by the krone of 100 heller in 1899. Since 1925 the schilling of 100 groschen has been used. Aluminium or aluminium bronze are used for the lower denominations, cupro-nickel for the schilling values and silver for occasional commemorative 25 or 50s pieces.

Belgium

The coinage of Belgium dates back no farther than 1830 when the country revolted against union with the Netherlands and became independent. Before that time Dutch, Spanish and French coins circulated in the Low Countries, and even earlier than that the rulers of Brabant, Hainault and Flanders, and the bishops of Liege minted their own coins. During and after the Second World War zinc-coated steel was used for Belgian coins ranging up to the 5-franc or 'belga' piece. Distinctive coins were also produced for use in the former Belgian Congo and included hexagonal pieces in brass featuring an elephant.

Bulgaria

An extensive coinage existed in the Middle Ages, when the Bulgarian Empire included much of the Balkans, and the coins were modelled on Byzantine pieces. The modern coinage, however,

Austria 1 kreuzer, 1858

Austria 10 groschen, 1952

Austria 5 schillings, 1958

dates from 1879 when Bulgaria won its independence from Turkey. Since then the 'lev' (plural leva) of 100 'stotinki' (literally 'hundredths') has been in use. Towards the end of the Second World War an iron coinage was introduced. The current series of the People's Republic consists of 1, 3 and 5s in bronze and coins from 10s to 1L in cupro-nickel. The common obverse shows the national coat of arms.

Bulgaria 50 stotinki, 1962

Bulgaria 5 stotinki
obverse: coat of arms,
reverse: numeral

Bulgaria 10 stotinki
obverse

Bulgaria 1 lev, 1962

Czechoslovakia

The first coins did not appear until 1921 and since then the 'korun' (crown) of 100 'haleru' has been used. The coins are struck in zinc, bronze or cupro-nickel but occasional commemorative pieces have been minted in silver. Separate coinage appeared during the Second World War in the puppet state of Slovakia and the German protectorate of Bohemia and Moravia, into which Czechoslovakia had been split.

Czechoslovakia 100
crowns: coat of arms

Denmark

Danish coins may be traced back to the silver pennies of Sweyn and Canute who ruled England and Norway as well as Denmark in the tenth century. The medieval coins of Denmark included a curious series inscribed in Latin and Hebrew. Since the creation of the Scandinavian Monetary Union in 1872 the 'krone' of 100 'ore' has been in use. Formerly silver and bronze were used for these coins but in more recent years zinc-coated steel, aluminium, cupro-nickel and brass have been used for coins ranging from the tiny 1 ore to the 2 kroner. A distinctive feature of Danish coins is the royal monogram on the obverse – an aid to identification on those coins (mid-nineteenth century) which do not include the name of the country. The small copper 'skillings' of that period bear the word RIGSMONT (State Mint).

Finland

Copper and silver coins were minted in 1917–18 by both Finnish nationalists and the Bolsheviks. Before the Russian Revolution the Tsars, as Grand-dukes of Finland, struck the 'markka' of 100 'pennia' depicting the imperial eagle. The coins of the republic replaced the eagle by the Finnish lion and this has continued down to the present day.

France

Space prevents more than a brief outline of the coinage of this country. During the Middle Ages many of the nobility struck their own coins. The royal coinage was reformed by Louis IX when the 'sou' was introduced. In the period prior to the Revolution French coinage became increasingly complex, with such units of currency as the 'ecu d'or', the 'angel' and the 'angelot', 'teston', 'pavillon d'or', 'louis d'or' and 'pistole'. During the Revolution money collapsed rapidly in value and coins were replaced by paper currency known as 'assignats' and 'mandats'. Napoleon introduced a decimal system of 100 centimes to the franc and this has remained in use ever since. The Napoleonic coins bore the portrait of the emperor or a crowned N. During the Second Empire (1852–71) the coins, in bronze, nickel or silver, portrayed Napoleon III with the French eagle on the reverse. After the downfall of the empire the female figure of Liberty replaced Napoleon. At the turn of the century Oscar Roty designed an obverse for the franc denominations, showing the female figure

Denmark 25 ore: crown
and royal monogram

Denmark 2 ore bronze
1889

Denmark silver rigsdaler,
King Frederick VII

Denmark 1 skilling

France silver coin of
Louis XVI 1788

Silver 5 francs of Louis
Philippe 1843

France 5 centimes 1917

France 5 francs ''Sower''
obverse

France 100 francs, 1954

France Vichy government
1 franc

French colonies Charles X
10 centimes, 1825

French Polynesia 2 francs

of a sower. La Semeuse, as she is known, appears on the nickel 1f and silver 10f coins down to the present time. Aluminium and aluminium-bronze coins have also been produced since the Second World War.

French Polynesia 50 francs

Greece

The modern coinage dates from the independence of Greece from Turkey in 1829 and is based on the 'drachma' of 100 'lepta'. The crown or coat of arms appears on the reverse and the portrait of the ruler on the obverse. The present series is cupro-nickel and ranges from 50l to 10dr with a portrait of King Constantine, although he has been in self-imposed exile for several years now.

Germany

One of the first acts of the newly established German Empire in 1871 was the introduction of a decimal currency based on the 'mark' of 100 'pfennige'. During the period down to the First World War the 1 and 2pf coins were struck in bronze, the 5 and 10pf in nickel and the higher denominations in silver. Gold 5, 10 and 20-mark pieces were also minted. The imperial double-eagle appeared on the obverse and the numerals of value on the reverse.

During the First World War 5pf coins were minted in zinc-coated steel, but inflation led to the rapid disappearance of all coins from circulation. From 1918 till the end of 1923 emergency money (notgeld) was issued in the form of paper notes, and thousands of different types were produced all over Germany, every town and village having its own currency. After the currency reform of 1924 bronze and silver coins were re-introduced. From 1936 onwards the Nazi swastika was incorporated in the designs. Lower denominations in the Nazi period were struck in aluminium bronze, but during the Second World War zinc was used for the 1, 2 and 5pf values. The coins issued during the Allied occupation were similar, but omitted the swastika emblem. Since 1948 two sets of coins have been in circulation. In the Federal Republic (West Germany) coins in bronze, aluminium-bronze or pure nickel are issued between 1pf and 5m, while the coins of the Democratic Republic (East Germany) are struck in aluminium. Both countries have also released commemorative coins from 5m upwards in silver.

Imperial Germany, obverse and reverse of 10 pfennigs 1894

Imperial Germany, obverse and reverse of 5 pfennigs

Prussia 4 groschen, 1804 obverse and reverse

Nazi Germany 5 marks obverse: Hindenburg, reverse: eagle and swastika

Greece 50 lepta obverse
and reverse George I

Hungary 50 filler obverse
and reverse

West Germany 5 pfennigs
1949

West Germany 1 mark,
obverse and reverse

West Germany 5 marks
pure nickel

East Germany aluminium
5 pfennigs obverse and
reverse 1949

Hungary

From the sixteenth century onwards, when Hungary was recovered from the Turks, the coinage of Austria was used. After the establishment of the dual monarchy in 1867 the coins of Austria-Hungary bore no inscription and circulated as 'kreuzers' or 'krajczars', depending on which part of the empire they were being used in. The korona of 100 'filler' was introduced in 1899, replacing the 'forint'. After the inflation of the early 1920s the currency was reformed and a new unit, the 'pengo', was introduced in 1925. This currency, in turn, was subject to astronomic inflation at the end of the Second World War and was replaced by the forint once more. The filler and 1 forint denominations are struck in aluminium while the 2fo and 5fo are minted in cupronickel. Various commemorative coins of 5fo upwards have been minted in silver.

Hungary 5 forint obverse:
Lajos Kossuth

Italy

The coins of modern Italy date from 1861, the year following the unification of the kingdom. The coins up to 10 'centesimi' were minted in bronze, while silver was used for the higher denominations. The profile of the king appeared on the obverse and the figures of value, in a wreath, on the reverse. Before the First World War the size of the bronze coins was greatly reduced and nickel was introduced for the medium denominations. The political development of Italy can be followed by the coins incorporating the fascist emblem, and the change in the king's title to RE E IMP (King and Emperor) after the annexation of Ethiopia in 1936. During the Second World War a type of stainless steel known as 'acmonital' (a word made up from the abbreviation of the three Italian words for 'Italian steel money') was introduced. Since the establishment of the republic in 1946 aluminium has been used for the 5 and 10 lire coins, stainless steel for the 50 and 100 lire coins and silver for the 500 lire. The attractive obverse and reverse designs—wheat-ears, rudder, porpoise, plough, blacksmith and female allegory of

Italy – are in the best tradition of the coins of Magna Graecia. Incidentally the Syracusan deka-drachm of the fifth century BC is reproduced on the current 500 lire banknotes.

Netherlands

An enormous range of different coins was circulated in the Netherlands from the Middle Ages till 1602 when some attempt was made to simplify the coinage. From that time a system of gold 'ducats', silver 'rijksdaalders' and bronze 'stuivers' and 'duits' was adopted. The French struck coins in the name of Louis Bonaparte as King of Holland from 1806 till 1814. Following the re-establishment of the Kingdom of the Nether-lands in 1815 a series of coins based on the 'gulden' or 'guilder' of 100 cents was introduced. Coins of the Netherlands continued to be minted at Brussels, till 1830 when the Belgian provinces seceded. Silver coins ranged from the crown-sized 2½g piece to the 25 cent denomination. At the present bronze is used for the 1 and 5c and nickel for the other denominations. The profile of the ruler appears on the obverse and a crown or the national coat of arms on the reverse. During the long reign of Queen Wilhelmina (1890–1948) five different portraits of her appeared on the coins. Zinc-coated steel was used for lower de-nominations struck during the German occupation in the Second World War.

Norway

Politically Norway was united with Sweden till 1905, but a separate coinage of 'ore' and 'kroner' was minted from 1872 onwards. Coins were struck in bronze or silver, the obverse featuring the lion emblem of Norway and the monogram of King Oscar II. The lion (obverse) and numeral (reverse) types continued in the series of Norway minted after independence in 1905. Iron and zinc were substituted for bronze and nickel or silver during the Second World War, though 10, 25 and 50 ore coins were struck at the Royal Mint, London for the Norwegian Government in Exile in 1942 and these were introduced in Norway itself after the country was liberated in 1945. The nickel coins, from 10 ore to 1 krone, originally had a central hole, but this has now been discontinued. Bronze 1, 2 and 5 ore coins are still minted. Like the coins of Denmark the Norwegian coins incorporate elements of Scandinavian ornament in their design.

Italy 20 centesimi, 1922 obverse and reverse

Italy 10 centesimi Umberto I obverse and reverse 1894

Italy 5 lire, Victor Emmanuel III obverse and reverse

Italian Republic 5 lire aluminium obverse and reverse

Italian Republic 10 lire, obverse: plough

Italian Republic 100 lire acmonital (steel) obverse: Italia, reverse: agriculture

Poland

Silver 'denars' were minted in Poland from the 10th century onwards and by the fourteenth century the coinage was closely modelled on that of western Europe, the French 'gros' becoming the standard unit in the reign of King Sygmunt (1506–48) and known in Polish as the 'groszy'. Gold coins ('zloty') were also minted. After the partitions of Poland at the end of the eighteenth century Austrian, Russian and Prussian coins were used, though the Free City of Cracow had its own 5 and 10g and 1z coins in 1835. Following the re-emergence of an independent Poland after the First World War the 'zloty' of 100 groszy was adopted. The series ranges from the zinc-coated steel of the lowest denominations to the 10z struck in silver. The Polish eagle and the numerals of value form the obverse and reverse designs.

Portugal

The modern coinage of Portugal was based on the 'reis'. The dollar-sized 800 reis coin known as the 'Portuguez da Prato' was equivalent to the Spanish eight-reales piece, and there were sub-divisions of 400 and 200 reis. The currency was reformed in the nineteenth century and the silver 'milreis' of 1000 reis introduced. After the establishment of the republic in 1910 a new currency was issued, based on the 'escudo' of 100 'centavos'. The lower denominations were struck in bronze and the higher values in silver, though cupro-nickel is now used for the latter. The five coats of arms arranged in the form of a cross, a reminder of the five Moorish kings defeated at the battle of Ourique in 1139, have been a common feature of the obverse of many Portuguese coins down to the present day.

Russia

Before Peter the Great modernised the coinage of Russia foreign gold and silver coins circulated widely. They were often melted down and cast into ingots known as 'grivny' – the name adopted as the unit of currency in the short-lived republic of the Ukraine at the end of the First World War. A half-ingot was known as a 'rouble', from the Russian verb 'rubit', to cut, and from this word came the unit of currency used in Russia to this day. To Russia goes the honour of having produced the first decimal currency in the modern sense, the rouble being tariffed at 100 'kopeks'

Netherlands 1 cent of Willem III, 1864

Netherlands 10 cents obverse and reverse 1953

Netherlands 5 cents 1950

Netherlands 25 cents obverse and reverse 1950

Netherlands 2½ cents, 1884

Tsarist Russia 5 kopeks obverse and reverse 1858

in the mid-eighteenth century. Coins in denominations of 3, 6 and 12 roubles were struck in platinum in 1828–30 for general circulation – the only example of this metal having been used other than in commemorative coins.

Spain

The modern coinage of Spain dates from 1866 when the real was replaced by the 'escudo' divided into 100 'centimos' or 1000 'milesimas'. Six years later the 'peseta' of 100 centimos was adopted and has remained in use to this day. The portrait of the ruler appeared on the obverse and the coat of arms on the reverse, a practice which has continued to the present, with a few notable exceptions. During the republican period of 1868–75 coins depicted a female figure and a lion, and included the weight of the piece in 'gramos' (reverse) and the number of pieces to the kilogram (obverse). Under the republic (1931–9) iron coins of 5 and 10c were struck. Since 1937 the Nationalist regime has struck coins with a profile of General Franco on the obverse.

Sweden

In 1624 Sweden produced cumbersome copper plates with the three crowns emblem and the royal monogram. This 'plate money' was superseded by a more orthodox type of coinage in 1759. Rectangular or diamond shaped silver coins known as 'klippe' were produced as a temporary issue in the sixteenth century. Before 1875 the unit of currency was the silver 'rigsdaler' divided into 48 'skilling banco' (up to 1858) or 100 'ore' (from 1858 onwards). The rigsdaler, about the size of an English shilling, was worth a quarter of the 'specie daler', a large crown-sized coin. In 1875 Sweden adopted the krone as the unit of currency. The present series ranges from the bronze ore to the cupro-nickel 2 'kronor'. The lower denominations feature the Swedish crown and have a numeral reverse, whereas the higher values bear the portrait of King Gustaf VI Adolf and the national coat of arms.

Switzerland

The federal coinage was introduced in 1850 and is based on the Swiss franc of 100 'rappen' or 'centimes'. This was modelled on the currency introduced by the French in 1798 for use in the

Tsarist Russia 2 kopeks 1814

Soviet Russia 3 kopeks obverse and reverse 1940

Spain 25 centinos pewter obverse and reverse

Spain 50 centinos General Franco

Spain 5 pesetas obverse and reverse 1949

Sweden 25 öre obverse and reverse, 1956

Helvetic Republic, but after the republic was dissolved in 1814 the individual cantons had returned to their own individual currency. The series of coins runs from 1 and 2c (bronze) and 5, 10 and 25c (cupro-nickel) to ½, 1 and 2 francs in silver. In 1968 cupro-nickel replaced silver for the franc denominations. The coins have a common reverse design, showing the value and date in a wreath. The obverses range from the Swiss cross and profile of Helvetia on the lower values to the standing figure of Helvetia on the franc denominations. Because there are four official languages in Switzerland (French, German, Italian and Romansch) Latin is used exclusively on the coins, the name of the country being rendered as HELVETIA or CONFOEDERATIO HELVETICA (Swiss Confederation).

Yugoslavia

Prior to the unification of this Balkan country in 1918 separate issues of coins were made by Serbia ('dinar') and Montenegro ('perper'), both units consisting of 100 'paras'. Montenegrin coins featured an eagle or portrayed Prince Nicholas I. Serbia's coins featured the double-headed eagle of the Karageorgevich dynasty and this was kept for the coins of Yugoslavia under the royalist government. The coins of the modern federative republic are inscribed in Roman or Cyrillic alphabets and sometimes in both. Up to 1966 the coins were minted in aluminium bronze and had various profiles symbolising agriculture and industry (obverse) and the coat of arms (reverse). In 1966 the currency was reformed, 1 new dinar of 100 paras being equal to 100 old dinars. The paras denominations are in aluminium bronze and the dinars in cupro-nickel, both having the coat of arms on the obverse and the figures of value on the reverse.

Space does not permit an outline of all the coin-issuing countries. Important series have been produced by the Vatican since 1929, continuing the privilege held by the Popes up to 1870 of striking their own coins. Other pocket states which have their own coins include Monaco, Liechtenstein and San Marino, though their currency systems are closely linked to France, Switzerland and Italy respectively and the coins of these countries circulate in those territories as well. Luxembourg, Albania and Roumania have also produced their own coins, as did the former Free City of Danzig from 1920 till 1939.

Switzerland 2 centimes obverse and reverse

Switzerland 20 centimes obverse and reverse

Yugoslavia 10 dinars obverse: agriculture

Yugoslavia 20 dinars obverse: industry

Yugoslavia 20 paras obverse and reverse

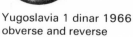

Yugoslavia 1 dinar 1966 obverse and reverse

Monaco 20 francs 1947

9
ASIAN COINS

The coin as we know it today is an Asiatic invention. At about the time the Lydians were coining electrum dumps the Chinese, at the other side of the continent, were producing small bronze articles which were used for the same purpose. These took the form of knives, spades, bill-hooks and other domestic implements, though the 'coins' could never have been used and did no more than symbolise an earlier form of barter currency. The knives are about six inches long and bear the value and the name of the issuing authority. The so-called 'pu' money, a modified form of the bronze spades, circulated widely in the fifth and fourth centuries BC. The Chinese used cowrie shells for small change and even went so far as to strike bronze replicas of cowries for use as money. Circular pieces of bronze, with a hole in the centre, first appeared in the fourth century BC and in 221 BC the emperor Shah Huang Ti first minted a regular series of half-ounce bronze coins. These remained in use for several centuries. In AD 618 the T'ang emperor Kau Tsu introduced the 'Kai-yuan' currency which remained in use till the beginning of this century. These coins, struck in bronze or brass, were circular and had a square hole in the middle. The four Chinese characters which appear on these coins signify 'current money of' and the appropriate reign. The copper cash of China, spanning a period of more than 2,000 years, is thus the world's longest lasting coinage.

Spanish, Mexican and British trade dollars circulated extensively and filled the need for coins of higher values. Towards the end of the nineteenth century China began minting its own silver coins, the 'Szechwan rupee' being the only coin to portray the Manchu emperor. Under the republic coins were struck with portraits of Dr Sun Yat-sen and Yuan Shih-kai. In the turbulent years of the 1920s various war-lords struck coins bearing their own portraits, while the Communist rebels of the 1930s produced rough coins portraying Lenin. The coins of the present-day Nationalist Republic portray Generalissimo Chiang Kai-shek and a map of Formosa. Communist China, however, continues an old Chinese tradition by using only paper money for all financial needs.

Western Asia

The Persians borrowed the idea of coinage from the Lydians in the sixth century BC. They minted silver 'sigloi' (shekels), twenty of which equalled a 'daric' of gold. An interesting feature of these coins was the use of a portrait of the reigning king – the first instance of living persons appearing on coins. In the third century BC the Parthians rebelled against the Seleucid kings who ruled Persia after the empire of Alexander the Great broke up. The Parthians struck silver drachmae and smaller copper coins with crude inscriptions in a mixture of Greek and Pehlevi script. Ardashir overthrew the Parthians at the beginning of the

China
copper cash

China, Nationalist
Republic aluminium coin

China, Nationalist
Republic brass
obverse Chiang Kai-shek
reverse Map of Formosa

Persia: drachm of Queen
Boran, 630–31 A.D.

Persia: gold stater of
Hormizd, 3rd–4th
century A.D.

third century AD and founded the Sassanian Empire. The Sassanid rulers coined in gold and silver and occasionally in copper. The portraiture on these coins was particularly fine.

The Arabs used the coins of neighbouring countries until the middle of the seventh century when Caliph Abd al-Malik introduced a coinage based on the gold 'dinar' (Denarius aureus), the silver 'dirhem' (drachma) and the bronze 'fils' (follis). To this day fils and dinars are used by many Arab countries and dirhems are used by modern Morocco. The teachings of Mohammed forbade the making of images so the Arab coins did not portray rulers living or dead. Instead great attention was paid to ornamenting with Arabic inscriptions, which often included quotations from the Koran. This Arab coinage was minted over a very wide area, from Spain and Morocco to the borders of China and India. By the twelfth century, however, many Arab coins were copying Byzantine models and some of them even portrayed Christ or the Virgin Mary! Kai Khusru II (1236–45) featured the lion and sun emblems of his wife, whose portrait he was forbidden to put on the coins.

In the thirteenth century the Mongols swept across Asia. The khans of the Golden Horde produced small silver coins, while the ilkhans of Persia struck large, handsome coins in gold, silver and bronze, reciting their titles and family tree in Mongol script. The Ottoman rulers of Turkey and western Asia began minting coins in the fifteenth century in gold, silver and bronze. The coins of the Ottoman sultans are comparatively monotonous, featuring the 'toughra' or monogram of the ruler and the inscriptions and numerals in Arabic. This type of coinage continued in Turkey until 1933 when the 'lira' of 100 'kurus' was adopted. The portrait of Kemal Ataturk, founder of modern Turkey, appeared on the coins and the inscriptions were henceforward given in the Roman alphabet.

Egypt, Morocco and the Yemen are other Arab countries which have produced their own coins over a long period, again favouring lengthy inscriptions in place of portraiture. In the present century, however, the portraits of rulers have been generally adopted. Though not geographically Asian it is convenient to group the coinage of North Africa with Asia since it is essentially Oriental in character. Among the modern issues, those of Libya and Tunisia are also worthy of note, with fine portraiture. In 1969 Tunisia issued a set of ten different silver dinars, each portraying President Bourguiba on the obverse and some

Sassanian Empire:
Ardashir I (226–240 A.D.)
silver drachma

Ottoman Empire bronze
coin obverse and reverse

Ottoman Empire silver coin
obverse and reverse

Libya 5 mils, King Idris

aspect of Tunisian history on the reverse.

Persian coins in modern times have followed the Arab pattern, but in the reign of the reforming Shah Nasr-ed-Din (1829–96) a central mint was established at Teheran using European machinery. Since then Persian coins have portrayed the ruler on the obverse and featured the lion and sun emblem on the reverse. Since the end of the First World War distinctive sets of coins have appeared in Syria, the Lebanon, Iraq and Saudi Arabia and, more recently, in the sheikdoms of the Persian Gulf. In 1964 Sharjah went so far as to issue a silver 5 rupee coin in memory of the late President Kennedy – no doubt with American collectors in mind.

India

It is likely that India evolved a form of coinage before the Greeks introduced their coins at the time of Alexander the Great. The earliest Indian coins were of silver or copper, relatively thick and often square in shape, with various symbols punched on both sides. The coins of the Hellenistic kingdom of Bactria from the second century BC onwards had inscriptions in both Greek and Prakrit script. The Kushans founded an empire in north-western India in the first century AD and their gold and copper coins remained current till the fifth century. In the tenth century various Hindu rulers founded petty kingdoms and minted their own coins, often depicting a seated goddess or a bull and horseman. In southern India the best known coinage was that of the Ardhras who used lead coins inscribed in native characters.

The Mogul rulers of India produced some attractive gold and silver coins from the fifteenth century onwards. The Arabic lettering on these coins is particularly fine. Often verses of Persian poetry were engraved on the coins, and sometimes the signs of the Zodiac were incorporated in the designs. From the beginning of the eighteenth century, however, the quality of the Mogul coins gradually deteriorated and many of the petty rulers began producing their own coins as the Mogul empire broke up. Under British rule many of the maharajahs and princes of India continued to strike coins in gold, silver or bronze for local use and this privilege was not abolished until 1947 when India became independent. The coins of India and Pakistan in more recent times are mentioned in Chapter 6.

Coins following Indian patterns have also been

Egypt 10 mils of King Farouk obverse and reverse

Liberia 25 cents bronze. Head of Liberty

Sharjah 5 rupees John F. Kennedy

Group of five gold mohurs featuring signs of the zodiac, 1605–27 A.D. Jahangir of India

used in Afghanistan, Nepal, Tibet and Bhutan. The modern issues of these states are, for the most part, minted in Europe.

The Far East

Japan introduced coinage from China in 708 and minted bronze coins from then until the middle of the tenth century. No imperial coins appeared from then until 1624 and the nobility filled the gap by issuing token coins. Copper 'kwan-ei' were produced in vast quantities from 1624 till 1869 when a mint on European lines was established and a currency based on the 'yen' of 100 'sen' introduced. Gold and silver pieces were minted from the sixteenth century onwards, ranging from the 'oban', a large oblong gold coin with rounded corners, and the little rectangular 'bu', to the so-called bean money struck in silver.

Korea adopted Chinese-style coins in the twelfth century. Towards the end of the nineteenth century an attempt was made to introduce silver coins, but shortly afterwards Korea was absorbed into the Japanese Empire. Distinctive Korean coins were re-introduced after the Second World War. In South Korea the currency has fluctuated violently in recent years. In 1953 the 'hwan' of 100 old 'won' was introduced, but nine years later the new won of 100 'chon', equal to 10 old hwan, was adopted. The coins are struck in aluminium and feature traditional emblems such as the rose of Sharon.

Until the middle of the nineteenth century Thailand (Siam) struck gold and silver in the form of balls or bullets bearing the stamp of the reigning monarch. Since 1850 coins on European lines have been produced, with portraits of rulers on the obverse. Gold, silver, nickel and bronze coins have been issued down to the present day. The native kingdoms of former French Indo-China – Annam, Cambodia and Laos – issued coins under French authority from 1860 onwards, with inscriptions in French and native characters. Since independence the coin types have varied considerably. South Vietnam, for example, mints 5 and 20 'dong' with scalloped or polygonal edges. Aluminium or nickel-coated steel are used in South Vietnam while aluminium and bronze are used for the 'xu' and 'hao' coins of North Vietnam.

Israel

Although the modern state of Israel has existed only since 1948 distinctive Jewish coins appeared

Portuguese India rupee of Don Luiz I, 1882 obverse and reverse

Indian Native States bronze and silver coins

Bhutan 3 rupees, 1966 obverse and reverse

Burma: bronze coin showing a peacock, the national emblem

Philippines 1 peso, 1908
obverse and reverse

Israel obverse and reverse
shekel of First Jewish
Revolt 66–70 A.D.

on two earlier occasions. In AD 66–70, during the so-called First Jewish Revolt against Roman rule silver 'shekels' and bronze half and quarter shekels were struck at Jerusalem. The coins featured religious emblems and fertility symbols, and the Hebrew inscription 'Freedom of Zion'. During the second Revolt (AD 132–5) shekels and 'denarii' were struck in silver, again featuring such symbols as a lyre or grapes. A large bronze coin was minted at the same time and depicted an amphora or wine jar. Various local coins were struck in such towns as Akko and Yafo in the third century AD.

The coinage of Israel made its debut in 1949 and was based on the 'pound' of 1,000 'pruta'. This was replaced in 1960 by the pound of 100 'agorot'. Since then coins have been minted in aluminium (1 agora), aluminium-bronze (5, 10 and 25 agorot) and cupro-nickel ($\frac{1}{2}$ and 1 lira or Israeli pound). Higher denominations of 5 and 10 'lirot' have been struck in silver or platinum for commemorative purposes. Many of the designs and inscriptions used on modern Israeli coins are drawn from earlier biblical models.

Africa

Apart from the countries of North Africa whose coins on account of their inscriptions are usually classed in the Asiatic group, few countries produced their own coins until quite recently. The independent republic of Liberia in West Africa has issued low-denomination cents featuring the head of Liberty closely modelled on contemporary American coins, but with a palm-tree reverse. Farther south the former French colonies of Dahomey, the Congo (Central African Republic) and Cameroun make joint issues of coins under the Central Bank of Equatorial Africa. The short-lived state of Katanga (Congo) issued coins depicting the copper crosses which were used as money before the introduction of coinage.

Equatorial Africa 25 francs,
obverse and reverse

COINS OF THE SASSANIAN DYNASTY OF PERSIA (224-651AD)

GOLD COINS OF JAHANGIR, MOGUL EMPEROR OF INDIA

Left to Right:
Drachm of Hormizd (272-273)
Drachm of Bahram II (276-293)
Gold Stater of Shapur II (310-379)
Drachm of Shapur III (383-388)
Drachm of Shapur I (241-272)

Below: Mohur showing Jahangir with
wine-cup (dated 1020AH/1611AD). Mohur
of the Lahore mint (1015). Mohur, zodiac
series, Aries (Agra, 1028AH). Mohur,
zodiac series, Taurus (Agra, 1028AH).
Mohur, zodiac series, Gemini (Agra,
1030AH). Mohur, zodiac series, Cancer
(Agra, 1029AH). Mohur, zodiac series,
Virgo (Agra, 1033AH).

10
COMMEMORATIVE COINS

Earlier chapters have looked at the scope of coin collecting according to the countries of origin. It is also possible to form a type collection, specialising in coins of a certain size or metal from different countries. Thus the dollars and crown-sized coins of the world have long enjoyed tremendous popularity with numismatists. On a humbler scale, however, excellent collections have been formed of shillings of Britain and the Commonwealth, or even the humble threepence, or 'joey' or 'tickey' as it is known in other countries. The appeal of crown-sized coins is obvious. On account of their large size they were never popular in everyday currency and thus they tend to have survived in better than average condition. Their large size has enabled medallists and engravers to produce many excellent designs. In

general their designs have been more artistic than is possible in coins of a smaller size. From this it naturally follows that the crown or dollar format is ideal for those special issues struck to commemorate famous persons and historic events.

The idea of minting coins for special occasions is not a new one. The famous dekadrachms of Syracuse were struck originally as prizes in the Assinarian and Demareteian Games. Some of these handsome coins even depict pieces of armour captioned 'athla' (prizes) and it is thought that the prizes were eventually converted into cash payments. It is unlikely that the dekadrachms circulated widely as coins, but would be intended to be kept and treasured by the recipients, just as Olympic medals are today. The Romans minted many so-called 'large brass' coins in the second and

Germany 5 and 20 mark
coins of 1913 celebrating
the centenary of the War
of Independence

Columbian Exposition half
dollar 1893 obverse
Columbus reverse *Santa
Maria*

Jamaica Commonwealth
Games crown, 1966

Bermuda crown 1964
obverse and reverse

third centuries AD to commemorate famous events. In 348 AD the thousandth anniversary of the foundation of Rome was celebrated by a lengthy series of coins tracing the history of the Eternal City.

In the Middle Ages gold 'augustales' were minted by the Holy Roman Empire for commemorative purposes and it is thought that the commemorative medal, evolved in Renaissance Italy in the fifteenth century, was inspired by these large and very attractive gold pieces. Commemorative medals developed all over Europe from the middle of the fifteenth century, for propaganda and satirical purposes, or to celebrate important anniversaries, or to pay tribute to outstanding men and women. At the same time, however, pieces with a nominal face value were minted for special occasions. Significantly it was in Germany, home of the thaler, that commemorative coins in the modern sense first appeared. Various states and cities, for example, struck thalers and half-thalers to celebrate the centenary and bi-centenary of the Lutheran Reformation. In the eighteenth and nineteenth centuries many thalers fell into the category of 'denkmunzen' (memorial money) and were intended for the collector's cabinet rather than general circulation. Many of the large coins produced by Austria and Switzerland were known as 'Schutzenfestmunzen' (shooting festival money) since they were awarded as prizes in the annual shooting competitions. The last of these coins minted by Austria was a thaler of 1868, but Switzerland has continued the

tradition down to the present and has minted as many as 30,000 pieces in more recent years.

The first coins in modern times to be minted in honour of a special occasion were the half and quarter dollars produced by the United States in 1893 to mark the Columbian Exposition in Chicago and the quatercentenary of the discovery of America by Columbus. Isabella of Spain was portrayed on the quarter, while Columbus and his flag-ship *Santa Maria* appeared on the half dollar. Since then the United States has produced many commemorative coins. Between 1893 and 1954 there were 48 half-dollars, one dollar and one quarter-dollar in silver and various gold coins. The practice got out of hand in the 1930s – in 1936 there were no fewer than 16 half-dollars alone – and some of the events commemorated were rather unimportant. No commemorative coins appeared in the United States till 1971 when a silver dollar honouring the late President Eisenhower was minted.

In Britain 'crowns' have not circulated in practice for many years, but since the Silver Jubilee of King George V in 1935 they have been released to celebrate coronations in 1937 and 1953, to mark the Festival of Britain (1951) and to pay tribute to Sir Winston Churchill (1966). Now that a 50p coin has been adopted it is not unlikely that this denomination could be used for commemorative purposes in future. Both Ireland and Guernsey issued commemorative ten-shilling coins in 1966, to mark the 50th anniversary of the Easter Rising and the ninth centenary of the

Tonga 2 pa'anga
Coronation of King George
Tupou IV 1967

Facing Page, Background Howick Falls in Natal, South Africa.
Top Left The wedding of Princess Elizabeth and Prince Philip, 1947
Top Right Fijian drummer
Below Sir Winston Churchill

Norman Conquest respectively. Canada has produced a number of commemorative silver dollars in recent years, and crowns have been issued by New Zealand, South Africa, Rhodesia, Zambia, Bermuda, Jamaica and other Commonwealth countries in recent years. New Zealand issued a commemorative half-crown in 1940 to mark the centenary of British annexation, while Australia issued commemorative florins.

Since the Second World War, and especially since 1960, the commemorative coin has increased enormously in popularity with collectors and this, in turn, has encouraged more and more countries to issue special coins. Among the commemorative coins of 1971 may be mentioned the following: Austria – 25 schilling Vienna Stock Exchange bicentenary, 50 schilling Julius Raab; Czechoslovakia – 50 koruny 50th anniversary of the Czech Communist Party; West Germany – 5 marks Beethoven bi-centenary; Iran – 25, 50, 75, 100, 200, 500, 750, 1000 and 2000 rials 2,500th anniversary of the Persian Empire; Iraq – 500 fils, 1 and 5 dinars 50th anniversary of the Iraqi Army;

Israel – 10 lirot 'Let My People Go'; and Canada – dollar marking the centenary of British Columbia.

An interesting development in recent years has been the release of coins simultaneously in several countries for the same object. In October 1968 eleven countries released coins to mark the anniversary of the Food and Agricultural Organisation of the United Nations. Among the issuing states were Bolivia, Burundi, Ceylon, Lebanon, Syria and Uganda. Subsequently special coins were issued by China, Cyprus, India, Iraq, Jordan, Philippines, Turkey and the United Arab Republic. In 1970 several territories – Antigua, Barbados, St Kitts, Dominica, Granada, Montserrat, St Lucia and St Vincent – issued four-dollar coins to mark the inauguration of the Caribbean Development Bank. A common obverse design was used for all eight coins, featuring sugar cane and a stem of bananas, with the slogan 'Grow more food for mankind'. These coins were therefore linked to the FAO coin project. Already quite a large collection could be made of coins publicising this Organisation, and it seems likely that there will be more to come.

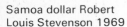
Samoa dollar Robert
Louis Stevenson 1969

Turks and Caicos
Islands, crown, 1969

Facing Page, Top Maori scene
in the North Island, New Zealand
Centre Left Vancouver's *Discovery*
as a convict ship
Centre Right Queen Victoria
and Prince Albert, 1861
Below King George VI, Queen Elizabeth
and Princesses Elizabeth and Margaret
acknowledge the cheers of the crowd
during Victory celebrations, 1945

11 TOKEN COINS

Strictly speaking any coin whose metal content is less than its nominal face value is a token, since a token is merely a promise or a symbol of something else which *has* real value. Paper money of all kinds is a token, as the inscription printed on banknotes implies – a promise 'to pay the bearer on demand'. At one time such a promise might have had real meaning and one could have demanded a gold sovereign in exchange for an English pound note, but as long as other people accept paper money in good faith, and give us goods or services in exchange, we do not trouble ourselves unduly about the token aspect of modern currency.

In less sophisticated societies, where people did not trust each other very much, money had to be seen to have a real value in itself. Thus precious metals were used for coins and even then an element of suspicion was always present. It was not uncommon for people to carry tiny pocket scales or balances so that they could check the weight of sovereigns and half-sovereigns received in change. People often tried to bite the edge of a coin to test its genuineness. Nowadays, however, we accept coins made of base metal, as well as paper money, and so long as the country has a stable economy we do not worry about the *real* value of coins.

In the numismatic sense a token is regarded as a substitute coin, produced in times when ordinary coins are scarce, or when there are economic or political crises. In most cases tokens were issued in place of base metal coins and were usually similar in weight and size to the denominations they replaced. In contrast, tokens have been made in silver, and even in gold, though the latter are very rare. The main difference between a token and a coin is that the former is issued by a bank or a private individual, whereas the latter is issued with the full authority of the country. Tokens only had a limited circulation, being confined in many cases to one locality or even one town. Their purpose was to supply the demand for small change, usually at a time when the government would not or could not produce the requisite coins.

Under the Roman Empire, for example, many towns and cities of Greece continued to strike copper coins for local usage. The small coins of Athens, Rhodes and other districts, referred to at the end of Chapter 2, were really tokens, though numismatists regard them as coins, so it is often difficult to know just where to draw the line.

Siege Tokens

Token coins have often been produced in times of war, when 'good money' has been hoarded and disappeared from circulation. The most interesting examples of wartime tokens are those produced in towns and cities under siege by the enemy. Leather tokens were used during the siege of Leyden in 1574, the bindings of books being cut up and stamped for use as money. Bronze sous were struck in the besieged cities of Antwerp and Strasbourg during the Napoleonic Wars. During the Civil War in England siege money was produced by the Royalists defending Newark, Carlisle, Colchester, Pontefract and Scarborough. Silver plate was melted down or cut up and stamped with the denomination. Some very unusual values were produced. Scarborough had tokens worth 7d and 3s 4d, and Newark produced a ninepenny piece. Lord Inchiquin produced some interesting tokens in Ireland in 1643. His silver tokens ranged in value from threepence to

half-crown and were stamped with their *weight*. He also issued a gold token stamped 4dwt. 7gr. on both sides, and passing current at the equivalent of the French pistole. This, incidentally, was the only gold coin ever struck in Ireland. The collector's term for such tokens is obsidional currency, from the Latin word *obsidium*, meaning a siege.

Tokens have often been produced in wartime, even if siege conditions are absent. Germany produced more than any other country during the First World War. Inflation drove silver coins out of circulation and the authorities recalled much of the bronze coinage which was then melted down to provide essential war materials. At first coins in iron, zinc or aluminium were issued by the government, but this measure failed to relieve the shortage of small change. In 1915, therefore, the government authorised banks, provincial and civic bodies to issue their own tokens, which could be redeemed for proper money whenever the return to peacetime conditions allowed. In fact the situation went from bad to worse and the 'notmunzen' (emergency coins) were replaced by 'notgeld' (emergency paper money) which depreciated faster than it could be printed. Nevertheless a few tokens continued to appear right up to the end of 1923 and it has been estimated that about 3,000 different tokens were produced in the eight-year period. They were mostly struck in iron, zinc or aluminium, but a few were made of porcelain, wood or card. They were produced by banks, trading companies, co-operative societies, public utilities such as railways, tramways and gas companies, chambers of commerce, provincial and civic bodies and even army units and prisoner-of-war camps. Many of these tokens were attractively produced, portraying famous persons associated with the town or district, or coats of arms and civic emblems.

Token coins were struck by traders in the United States during the Civil War (1861–5) and by France, Belgium and other countries during the First World War. The United States also hit upon the idea of encasing postage stamps in small discs and using them as tokens of the equivalent value. This idea was resurrected by France, Germany, Austria and other countries during and immediately after the First World War. Tradesmen used the back of the discs for advertisements, while the stamp could be seen through a plastic window. Encased postage stamps were also issued by the banks instead of metal tokens.

Russia and the Ukraine took the idea a stage farther and printed postage stamps on thick card,

USA bronze token 1863

France brass 20c token
1922

Belgium 25c tramways
token obverse and reverse

Germany 5/100th
emergency mark 1923

Germany 1/10th
emergency mark obverse
and reverse 1923

with an inscription on the back to show that the 'stamps' were on par with silver currency. Stamps stuck on special cards were used as money in Rhodesia at the time of the Boer War and by Spain during the Civil War of 1936–9.

Tradesmen's Tokens

Token coins have also been produced in peace-time when the government has failed to issue coins at various times. In Britain, for example, tokens have been produced on three separate occasions when copper coins were not issued by the authorities. During the Civil War, and subsequently under the Commonwealth, the value of money fell and there was a need for base metal coins to replace the silver penny, as well as to meet the need for halfpence and farthings. The government, however, refused to issue copper coins and it was not until the re-coinage after the Restoration of Charles II that halfpence and farthings were issued. In the meantime it was left to tradesmen and inn-keepers to issue their own tokens. In the twenty-six years when the tokens were used some 15,000 to 20,000 different types were produced. Token halfpence and farthings were also issued by towns and villages, by the church authorities and manufacturers. Many of these tokens were very simple, often bearing no more than the initials of the issuer and the date. Oblongs, squares, diamonds and hearts as well as circles were produced. These tokens were issued in copper, brass, pewter or lead. The practice of issuing tokens was suppressed by royal proclamation in August 1672, though some years passed before they died out altogether.

In the eighteenth century copper coins were minted from time to time, but there was never enough to satisfy the needs of the people. No copper coins were minted at all between 1775 and 1797 when the 'cartwheels' of Boulton and Watt were issued. In 1787 the Parys Mine Company of Anglesey began minting halfpennies and pennies from locally mined copper. The obverse of these tokens portrayed a Druid, as Anglesey had been the last stronghold of the Druids in Britain. These tokens became very popular and quickly spread all over England and Wales. Soon they were being imitated by other tokens and by the end of the century the number of different types was astronomical. Unlike their seventeenth century predecessors these tokens were often finely produced and highly artistic in their designs. While many of them were genuinely produced by

Britain 1793 token
farthing, South Wales

Britain Bristol & South
Wales penny

Britain Lackington
halfpenny

Britain Anglesey ''druid''
halfpenny

Britain 1812 token
halfpenny

Lancaster halfpenny
token, featuring John of
Gaunt 1797

Britain East India House
halfpenny

North Wales halfpenny
token, 1793

Bath penny token 1811

Colour Plates

I. United Kingdom

(a) Shilling of King Charles I with motto "Christ enlarge the Kingdom"
(b) Britannia reverse of the penny of 1806
(c) Guernsey ten shillings portraying William the Conqueror, 1966
(d) Twelve-sided threepence showing a portcullis, 1967
(e) Twelve-sided threepence of Jersey showing the coat of arms of the bailiwick, 1964
(f) Silver florin of 1935
(g) Silver threepence of 1935
(h) Silver sixpence of 1910
(i) Bronze penny of 1967
(j) Bronze farthing of 1951 depicting a wren
(k) Silver halfcrown of 1915

II. Europe, Africa and Asia

(a) Austria schilling showing an edelweis, the national flower
(b) Denmark 2 kroner depicting the Crown
(c) Russia 5 kopeks bronze coin of 1769 with monogram of the Tsarina
(d) Ottoman Empire bronze coin of the late nineteenth century
(e) France coin portraying Marianne, allegory of the republic
(f) France 25 centimes coin of 1923
(g) Imperial Germany, bronze pfenning showing the imperial eagle
(h) Yugoslavia 50 dinars, 1955
(i) Katanga 5 francs, 1961, showing a Katanga copper cross, a primitive form of currency
(j) Spain, 5 pesetas showing the national coat of arms
(k) Nazi Germany 5 reichsmarks, 1934
(l) Denmark bronze coin with monogram of King Christian X

III. Crown-sized Coins

(a) Isle of Man silver crown of 1970 showing a tail-less cat
(b) New Zealand dollar showing Captain James Cook, 1969
(c) South Africa silver crown commemorating the tercentenary of Van Riebeeck's landing, 1952
(d) Great Britain obverse of the silver crown, with profile of King George VI
(e) Great Britain obverse of the Jubilee crown, 1887, with profile of Queen Victoria
(f) Great Britain Churchill commemorative crown, 1966
(g) Great Britain Coronation crown, 1953: Queen Elizabeth on horseback
(h) New Zealand cupro-nickel dollar, 1967

IV. Tokens

(a) and (c) Spanish Civil War cardboard tokens with stamps to indicate values of 25c and 15c
(b) Montreal, Canada, token sou (halfpenny)
(d) Scottish communion token, Avondale Parish, 1850
(e) Canadian "ship" token halfpenny
(f) Great Britain model coin for an improved coinage system, mid-nineteenth century
(g) Canada, Hudson's Bay Company, $\frac{1}{2}$ "made beaver" token
(h, i, l) United States traders tokens of Prescott, Nevada, and Teller City, Alaska, nineteenth century
(j) France 5c encased postage stamp token, 1919
(k) Great Britain Co-operative Society token for threepence

merchants and businessmen for use as small change, many others were produced primarily for advertising purposes. The so-called tradesmen's 'tickets' provide a valuable insight into the commercial world of the late eighteenth century, giving us the names, addresses and specialities of shopkeepers and manufacturers all over the country. A number of tokens were produced mainly for sale to collectors and these include the most elaborate types, depicting churches, bridges, prominent landmarks and works of art. Sometimes these tokens were sold in sets and they were even produced by collectors for exchanging with other collectors. There were also the so-called mail-coach halfpence, depicting coaches and famous inns or paying tribute to John Palmer who was responsible for the introduction of the first mail-coaches in 1784.

The cartwheel coins of 1797 did little to satisfy the demand for tokens and they continued to appear throughout the Napoleonic Wars. After the Great Recoinage of 1816 tokens were declared illegal and rapidly disappeared from circulation. Silver tokens, in denominations of eighteen pence and three shillings, were issued by the Bank of England in 1811 and this practice quickly spread. Silver tokens of smaller denominations were issued in Ireland and the Channel Islands. They were also issued by private individuals, mainly to pay the wages of their workpeople.

The last phase of British tokens came in the 1820s and early 1830s and reflected the social and economic condition of the country following the Napoleonic Wars. Tokens were issued by public bodies, institutions and workhouses and could be exchanged for meals, lodging or goods. Benevolent societies and trade unions also struck tokens and many of these are of great interest to the social historian. Factory and mine owners often struck tokens which could be exchanged by their workers at the factory shop or canteen. This practice was open to abuse and was expressly forbidden by the various Truck Acts of the 1830s. Tokens in various forms have survived to the present day. Co-operative societies and grocers often produce tokens in metal or plastic and give 'checks' as a form of discount to their customers.

Tokens have been produced in many countries, either during a shortage of government coinage, or in the period before proper coins were adopted. Australia, New Zealand and Canada had extensive token coinages before their own distinctive coins were introduced. The Canadian tokens, in particular, were interesting and common, being pro-

Britain John Palmer
mailcoach token

Ireland 10d. silver token
1805

Ireland 10d. silver token
1813

duced by the various banks and also by the Hudson's Bay Company. The brass tokens issued by the latter represented beaver skins and were issued in denominations from an eighth to one 'made beaver'. Australia had 'kangaroo' copper tokens in the early nineteenth century. Copper tokens were produced in vast quantities in England for circulation in Canada and some of these had a propaganda element, such as the 'Ships, Colonies and Commerce' halfpence used in Prince Edward Island which referred to the three factors winning the war for Britain over Napoleon.

Brass tokens worth 50 centimes, and 1 or 2 francs, were issued in France during the 1920s by the Chamber of Commerce during the economic crisis of that period. These tokens bore the inscription BON POUR (good for). Incidentally popular nicknames for tokens are 'goodfors' and 'bonpours'.

Britain 3 shillings silver token 1813

Lower Canada halfpenny 1837

$\frac{1}{8}$th ''made beaver'' token, Hudson Bay Co. obverse and reverse

Quebec sou (halfpenny) token 1852

$\frac{1}{4}$ ''made beaver'' token reverse

Nova Scotia halfpenny 1832

France brass 1 franc token 1922–23

12
OTHER
KINDS
OF COINS

The tokens mentioned in the previous chapter all have one thing in common – they were intended as coins and had a value applied to them. There have been other kinds of token, many of which should really be regarded as tickets though struck in metal and having the appearance of tokens or coins. Other tokens are produced for a variety of reasons when some form of substitute for coins is desirable, but the tokens are not meant to circulate as coins.

Admission Tokens

Tickets made of pasteboard or card are a relatively modern invention. In the eighteenth and nineteenth centuries it was customary to use metal for this purpose. Tokens were struck in bronze, brass

101

or pewter and used as tickets of admission to pleasure gardens, such as Ranelagh or Vauxhall near London, to public entertainments, exhibitions, fairgrounds and theatres. Some of the theatre tokens were struck in silver and were designed as season tickets, being engraved with the name of the token-holder and often including the number of his seat or box.

Communion Tokens

A specialised form of admission token was the metal piece struck in connection with the annual sacrament of Communion in Presbyterian churches. Communion tokens had their origin in Scotland, though numerous examples were produced by Protestant churches in France, the Netherlands, South Africa, the United States and various Commonwealth countries. Tokens made of lead were introduced at the beginning of the seventeenth century, though most eighteenth and nineteenth century examples were produced in pewter and occasionally in bronze or brass. The earliest types had a crude inscription on one side only, but eventually they became quite elaborate, with Biblical texts, the name of the parish and the date. Some tokens even incorporated the coat of arms of the town or parish, or attempted to depict the church itself. The Communion Cup and the Burning Bush, symbol of the Church of Scotland, were common features on many of the later tokens. Circular, oval or lozenge-shaped tokens were the commonest types, though diamonds and hearts have also been recorded. The use of metal tokens has virtually died out in Scotland, but continues to this day in other countries, especially Canada and the United States, where some very attractive pictorial tokens have been issued in recent years, often commemorating important anniversaries of a church.

Jetons and Counters

'Jetons' (from the French word *jeter*, to throw) were produced from the thirteenth century onwards for use in accountancy. Royal jetons were produced by Philip the Bold and were used by the clerks of the royal exchequer in France for computing taxes and revenues. This practice was soon adopted by the French nobility who struck jetons bearing their coats of arms and insignia. Jetons were produced in gold, silver, brass or copper. In the seventeenth and eighteenth centuries they were manufactured in vast quantities and used

Scottish Communion tokens early 19th century

One-armed bandits or fruit machines
in a gaming saloon in Las Vegas

widely by tax inspectors all over Europe. In modern times jetons have been found useful, in times of fluctuating currency, for telephone kiosks and slot machines, the jetons being sold at the prevailing rate for the period.

Gaming Tokens

Jetons, jacks, chips and counters are also used in various games of chance. A type popular in Britain is a brass piece resembling the golden guinea of the eighteenth century, with a profile of the king on one side and the royal coat of arms on the other. These tokens were inscribed 'In memory of the good old days', but it is likely that

some illiterate people may have been taken in by them and accepted them as coins. They were intended primarily as gambling counters and must have been very popular, judging by the number which still exist. In the early nineteenth century another popular item was the 'Cumberland Jack', an imitation sovereign struck in brass with a crowned horseman replacing the familiar St George and Dragon. The inscription 'To Hanover' is the clue to the identity of this piece. Under Salic Law (this stated that a male heir must always take precedence) Queen Victoria could not succeed to the Hanoverian throne, and her place was taken by her unpopular uncle, Prince George, Duke of Cumberland. It is thought that the Cumberland

Jack was produced as a satirical piece, but it was often passed off as a genuine sovereign on the unsuspecting public.

In the United States silver dollars were widely used as gaming counters, but by the early 1960s they were rapidly disappearing from the scene. Since 1964 they have been replaced by cupro-nickel or nickel-brass gambling tokens of the same size most of which are struck by the Franklin Mint of Yeadon, Pennsylvania. Each casino has its own distinctive type of token and many of the designs are attractive. Franklin tokens are now used in many of the gaming clubs and casinos of Britain and Europe. Small brass tokens are also produced for use in 'one-armed bandits' and 'fruit machines' and a surprisingly large and interesting collection could be formed of the different types.

Model Coins and Toy Money

Sooner or later most collectors come across small items which look like coins yet were never put into circulation. Joseph Moore, a Birmingham manufacturer, produced a model coinage consisting of small bronze coins with a plug of silver in the centre. These model coins, portraying Queen Victoria, were designed as a means of improving the coins used in nineteenth century Britain. Similar model coins were produced by H. Hyams and had a brass centre in a bronze surround, and ranged from the crown (about the size of a current British 2p coin) to the halfpenny. A tiny bronze coin was produced in 1887 with Victoria's profile on one side and St George and the Dragon on the other. The inscription 'Jubilee Model Half Farthing' indicates its commemorative nature. Another commemorative item is the diminutive silver piece portraying the infant Prince of Wales (later King Edward VII) struck as a toy coin shortly after his birth in 1841. Model and miniature coins of this sort were popular in Christmas crackers during the nineteenth century.

Tiny replicas of current coins have also been produced in many countries for use as toy or dolls' money. At present there is little numismatic interest in these pieces, though not so long ago I was shown an impressive array of these miniatures by a collector in Melbourne. Toy money, for teaching children arithmetic, is also worth considering. During the transitional period from sterling to decimal currency in Britain many different types of instructional money were produced, in plastic or metal, and these are worth collecting as a memento of the greatest currency reform in Britain since Roman times.

Obverse and reverse of Jubilee half farthing model coin. Obverse Queen Victoria, reverse St. George

Model coin by H. Hyams, bronze with brass centre

Using gaming tokens
in an American casino
(*The Only Game in Town*)

13
COLLECTING COINS AND TOKENS

Coin collecting, like charity, should begin at home. In most cases collectors are first attracted to the hobby by studying the coins of their own country, since these are most readily available. This has long been the custom in the United States and Canada, for example, where collectors seldom had the chance to pick up ancient or foreign coins. In Britain and the European countries the more serious collectors concentrated on the coins of Greece and Rome and tended to neglect the coins of their own land. In recent years, however, the craze for change-checking has spread to Britain and Europe and this was stimulated in Britain by the introduction of decimal currency over the period from 1968 to 1971.

The British collector is particularly fortunate in having such a wide range of material to choose from. He is fortunate to have a coinage, still in circulation, which dates so far back. Theoretically silver coins from 1816 and bronze coins from 1860 could still turn up in change, though it is unlikely that the earlier coins would be found in anything but very worn condition. In many countries the dates on the coins are changed at infrequent intervals, but in Britain coins were usually dated according to the year in which they were minted. As a result many of the commoner coins, such as pennies and shillings, were released with a new date each year. If one searches hard enough, it is possible to put together a collection of pennies, showing each date from 1860 to 1967, merely by picking them up in change. Of course many of the earlier 'bun' pennies would not be in very good condition and would be almost worthless from a collector's viewpoint. More on the subject of condition, and its relation to the value of coins, will be said in the next chapter.

In the United States Indian Head and Lincoln cents have been in use for many years and offer a wide range of dates. To the serious numismatist date-collecting seemed a rather infantile pastime, but there can be no doubt that this method of collecting encouraged a deep interest in modern coins and formed a useful apprenticeship for the budding collector. Many American coins, from the cent to the half-dollar, have been in circulation for a century or more, but here again, the earlier dates are not likely to turn up in fine condition, unless they have been hoarded for a considerable time.

Visits to foreign countries will yield a good crop of coins, and it is interesting to see what coins are in circulation and how often they turn up. Why is it, for example, that Italy can get by with no more than four coins (5, 10, 50 and 100 lire) and the United States with five (1, 5, 10, 25 and 50 cents), while Britain has seven ($\frac{1}{2}$, 1, 2, 5, 10 and 50 as well as the sixpence) and Bulgaria has eight (1, 3, 5, 10, 20, 25 and 50 stotinki and 1 lev)? The average number of different denominations seems to be six for all practical purposes. Very small and very large coins tend to be unpopular, either because they get lost easily or because they are too cumbersome to carry around in one's pocket or purse.

Much can also be learned from the type of metal used. Look at the difference between the flimsy aluminium coins of East Germany and the solid, heavy, prosperous looking brass and nickel coins of West Germany. Silver coins may still be found in circulation in a number of countries, including France, Britain, Canada and the United States, though in most cases these precious metal coins are rapidly disappearing into collections or being recalled by the banks for melting down.

Another interesting point about travel abroad is to discover to what extent the coins of other countries are used beyond the country of origin. Visitors to the Isle of Man, for example, will find that island's distinctive coinage circulating alongside the coins of the United Kingdom and the Republic of Ireland. Irish coins are used freely in Ulster and British coins in Eire. United States coins are frequently found in circulation in Canada, Mexico and many of the West Indian islands alongside the indigenous coinage. Australian coins circulate in New Zealand and are identical in size and shape to the New Zealand coins, with the exception of the 2 cent piece. Slot machines in New Zealand carry a warning that Australian 2c coins must not be used since they would jam the machine. In certain parts of the Netherlands Belgian or German coins are in common use as well as Dutch coins. Collecting coins in the countries one visits can teach a lot about the economy of the country and the commercial contacts it has with its neighbours.

We can also learn a lot from the coins themselves. Pre-war Russian coins bore an inscription 'Workers of the world unite', but such political slogans have long since disappeared from the Soviet coins. The swastika and the fasces were featured on the coins of Nazi Germany and Fascist Italy in the 1930s but the emblems of dictatorship are now absent from the world's coins. Female figures are popular subjects for coins, and in this we may see the image which a country wishes to show to the world at large. Many countries of the American continent favour the figure of Liberty, a reminder perhaps of their hard-won freedom from the former European colonial powers. The European countries, on the other hand, have a wider range and usually their ladies present a more warlike appearance. Britannia for centuries has appeared with a shield and naval trident, symbolising mastery of the sea. It is significant that the Britannia on the 50 pence coin now holds forth an olive branch and the sea has been left out of the design! The female figures of industry, commerce, agriculture, justice and harmony who grace the coins of Europe are the direct descendants of the goddesses who appeared on Greek and Roman coins.

The inscriptions on coins are often revealing. Latin, once universal, has virtually disappeared from the coins of the world, except those of Switzerland as already mentioned, and those of Britain. The inscription on British coins has shrunk considerably since the eighteenth century when the king had so many titles that they were reduced to a string of meaningless Latin abbreviations. If we examine the coins of the first Georges we would find this inscription on the obverse: M.B.F. ET H. REX F.D. B. ET L. D. S.R.I.A.T. ET E. In full this would have read *Magnae Britanniae, Franciae et Hiberniae Rex; Fidei Defensor; Brunswick et Luneburg Dux; Sancti Romani Imperii Archi-Tresorius et Elector* – King of Great Britain, France and Ireland, De-

fender of the Faith, Duke of Brunswick and Luneburg, Arch-Treasurer of the Holy Roman Empire and Elector. The coat of arms on British coins of this period showed four shields bearing the lions of England and Scotland, the harp of Ireland, the fleur-de-lys of France and the horses of Brunswick, Luneburg and Hanover. It is hardly surprising that relations between Britain and France were always so bad. The reference to France and the fleur-de-lys were tactfully dropped at the time of the recoinage in 1816, and later the inscription OMN BRITT (*Omnium Brittanorum*) was adopted to signify 'of all the Britons'. F.D. or FID DEF was added to the coins after the Pope had granted King Henry VIII the title of 'Defender of the Faith'. Though Henry later fell out with the Pope he held on to the title and it appears on the coins of Britain to this day. D.G.R. or DEI GRATIA REX (REG) signifies 'By the Grace of God, King (Queen) and is also retained to this day. British coins from 1893 till 1948 incorporated the abbreviation IND IMP (Empress or Emperor of India).

The British rulers were not the only ones who laid claim to more territory than was their right. French kings proclaimed themselves rulers of FR ET NAV (France and Navarre – though much of the latter forms part of Spain). Not to be outdone the kings of Spain in turn proclaimed themselves rulers of HISPANIARUM ET INDIARUM – 'the Spains and the Indias'. Nowadays, however, coins are simpler in their inscriptions which are usually confined to the name of the country and the value.

Buying Coins

Sooner or later the collector will tire of merely picking up coins in change. There will be annoying gaps in the collection – elusive dates and coins which are not available in really good condition. To fill these gaps he must eventually go to a dealer. Not many years ago there were no more than a handful of coin dealers in Britain and the major cities of Europe, though collectors in America were more fortunate. With the boom in coin-collecting in recent years the number of dealers has grown enormously and it is estimated that there are now over 300 full-time dealers in England and Wales alone. The number of actual shops is still small, since the majority of dealers prefer to do business by post. If you want to find the nearest dealer consult the yellow pages in the telephone directory, or look at the advertisements in one of the coin magazines. Many dealers publish lists of the coins they have for sale and these are sent out regularly to their customers. Buying by post is fairly satisfactory, though it may work out rather expensive since coins sent by post have to be registered. Most of the coin shops in Britain are in the London area, although many of the larger towns now have a shop, perhaps an antique dealer or stamp dealer, who also handles coins, tokens and medals. The advantages of buying coins over the counter are obvious; you can examine the dealer's stock and make your choice from the available coins and can be satisfied as to their condition. Coins turn up in the unlikeliest places – junk shops, church bazaars and jumble sales are always worth a visit and some very important and valuable finds have come to light in this way.

The most important source of coins nowadays is the auction. Many of the best collections and rarest coins are disposed of by auction, but this is also the place where bargains are to be found and may be the best method of buying a small collection to form the basis of a much larger one. In Britain the only auctioneer specialising in coins is Glendinning's, but both Sotheby's and Christie's hold coin sales at frequent intervals, and several of the provincial auctioneers also handle coins and medals. In Europe the leading auctioneers include Jacques Schulman of Amsterdam, Münzen und Medaillen of Basle and Hess-Leu of Lucerne.

Sales are held at the Hotel Drouot in Paris and the Dorotheum in Vienna. In America the leading firms are Hans Schulman and Stack's, both of New York and Dunn's of Norfolk, Virginia. Much of the bidding in auctions is done by post, but there are so many pitfalls about buying at auction that it is advisable to get one of the coin dealers to bid on your behalf. Most dealers do this for a small commission.

Exchanging Coins

All collectors inevitably accumulate unwanted coins or duplicates of those already in their collections. These coins can very often be exchanged with other coin collectors and new items added to the collection in this way. Collectors frequently advertise in the magazines, stating what they have for sale or exchange and what sort of coins they themselves are looking for. Most towns now have a coin club or numismatic society. By joining a club you have the chance to meet other collectors and swap coins. Your public library will tell you the clubs there are in the district, while local newspapers often report meetings. Not only will you have the opportunity to add to your collection, but you will learn a great deal from contact with other collectors. Many of the larger clubs have a junior section, or have school coin clubs affiliated to them.

Brass pocket coin balance
for checking the weight
of sovereigns and half-sovereigns

14
THE CONDITION AND VALUE OF COINS

Collectors often wonder what it is that makes a coin valuable. If it is made of gold or silver a coin will have a certain value even if it is in very poor condition. Theoretically at least it will have a scrap value, although it is against the law in many countries to melt down coins for their metal content. If you look at a coin catalogue, however, you will often find that the metal content of a coin has little or no bearing on its value to a collector. In such cases other factors have to be considered. The law of supply and demand applies to coins and tokens as to any other collectable object. The humble farthing provides a good example of this. Fewer than two million were minted in 1956, the last year in which they were issued. This was the smallest number of farthings produced since 1892 and being also the last date in use the 1956 farthing was eagerly snapped up by collectors, with the result that today one of these coins would cost up to £1 in uncirculated condition – almost a thousand times more than its face value.

The story of the last of the old halfpennies is rather different. The last date to appear on this coin was 1967 and when it was announced that year that there would be no more halfpennies collectors, remembering the sharp rise in the value of farthings, snapped them up very quickly. People were investing in sealed £5 bags and for a time there was a brisk trade in shiny new 1967 halfpennies at ten times their face value. Then the government announced that, to cope with the demand from collectors, the minting of 1967 half-pennies would continue indefinitely. As a result more than 100 million halfpennies were even-tually struck – more than any other halfpenny ever minted. Far from being a scarce coin the 1967 halfpenny is the commonest of its kind and always will be, since there was virtually no need for halfpennies by 1967 and most of these coins will have been kept in uncirculated condition.

As a rule the collector should not worry unduly about the number of coins issued. The issue of most modern coins is astronomical, usually run-ning into millions, so that there are always plenty to go round. It is significant that when the last farthing appeared no one bothered about it since there were far fewer collectors in 1956 than there were ten years later. It is seldom wise to collect coins merely as a form of investment.

The value of coins depends to a large extent on their popularity with collectors. Certain countries are more popular than others and there is likely to be fierce competition for the coins of the more fashionable countries, like the United States, Canada or France, especially if there is plenty of variety, different dates, dies and mint-marks. Even within one country certain periods may be more popular than others and this will be reflected in the value of the coins. Surprising as it may seem, in Britain the coins of Queen Elizabeth's reign, in uncirculated condition, had a steeper rise in value than similar coins of earlier reigns, merely because most of the new recruits to the hobby were interested in coins of the present day. This is not so extreme, now that the obsolete shillings and pence have gone out of circulation, and the

A machine for roll-wrapping coins at the new Royal Mint, Glamorgan, South Wales

value of Elizabethan coins of the period 1953–67 has tended to level off.

The subtle differences in coins can make a vast difference in value. The date on a coin is an obvious difference and, depending on the number of coins minted in a particular year, the value may be seriously affected. In Britain there were only 120,000 pennies dated 1951 and an example in uncirculated condition would today cost at least £10 ($25). No pennies appeared in 1952 and then there were 1,308,400 struck in 1953. Being a coronation year this date was in great demand and therefore a 1953 uncirculated penny is today worth between £2 ($5) and £3 ($7.50). No more pennies were minted until 1961 when there were over 48 million. Consequently a 1961 penny in uncirculated condition is today worth about 20p (50c).

Sometimes you will come across coins of the same date but bearing different mint-marks. Fortunately this problem has seldom occurred on British coins, though it is frequently found on American coins. In 1918, during the First World War, the Royal Mint produced over 84 million pennies but as this quantity was not enough two outside contractors were given the task of striking pennies also. Between them, the King's Norton Mint and Heaton & Co, both of Birmingham, produced 3,660,800 pennies in 1918 and 5,209,600 in 1919. In both years tiny letters were added to the design beside the date, either H or KN, the latter being the scarcer for both years. The Heaton mint also produced pennies in 1912 and these are distinguished from the ordinary Royal Mint coins by the letter H beside the date. Even in poor condition there is quite a difference in the value of the coins with these mint-marks and the corresponding dates without. A 1918 penny in fairly worn condition would be worth about 10p (25c); the same penny with the H mint-mark would be worth about 40p and one with the KN mint-mark about 50p ($1.25). In brilliant uncirculated condition the corresponding values would be £12 ($30), £70 ($175) and £120 ($300). This indicates the difference in value not only between the various mint-marks but in the various degrees of condition, of which more is said later.

Normally a coin is struck from two dies, an obverse die and a reverse die. Occasionally more than one die may be used for each side, differing in some slight detail. A good example of this is provided by the British 1902 penny whose reverse dies differ in the position of the horizontal line of the sea. These coins are nick-named 'high tide' and 'low tide' pennies for this reason. The low tide penny is the scarcer of the two and is worth four times as much as the high tide variety. The halfpennies of 1954–67 had two different obverse dies and twelve different reverse dies. Because the same pair of dies was not always used the number of possible combinations of obverse and reverse is 23. Fortunately not all these combinations appeared in any one year, though in 1967, for example, there were four possible types of halfpenny, two of which are very common while one is scarce and the other a major rarity.

Coins sealed in
a transparent plastic sleeve
for protection

You need to have very good eye-sight, or a high-powered magnifying glass to spot the differences in these dies. The difference in the obverses lies in the number of beads in the circular border; one has 110 beads and the other 111. The two reverses used in 1967 are almost identical, but the right-hand flag on one type has had the lines recut and strengthened. The common combinations are: 110 beads plus recut flag, and 111 beads plus weak flag. The scarce combination is 111 beads plus recut flag, while the very rare one is 110 beads plus weak flag.

Condition

Coins are fairly hard-wearing things. They have to be, since they pass from hand to hand, jingle in pockets and purses, rattle through slot-machines and get mistreated in many other ways. How hard-wearing they are is shown by the number which has survived for hundreds, if not thousands, of years. Nevertheless there are various degrees of wear and tear and often they have an effect on the value of a coin. This is particularly true of modern coins which are plentiful in fine condition. In such cases the collector should always strive for the best and never be content with coins in worn condition. Older coins are harder to find in excellent condition and the collector will often have to make do with coins showing some signs of wear. Collectors have worked out a system for describing coins and this is used in catalogues and advertisements, so it is important to understand exactly what is meant.

PROOF   A coin struck from special dies, usually with a high mirror finish, and sometimes in a more precious metal than the normal coin (e.g. silver instead of cupro-nickel). Proofs are produced mainly for sale to collectors and are not intended for circulation. They are often issued in attractive plush-lined cases or sealed in special boxes to preserve them from the effects of handling.

FLEUR DE COIN or BRILLIANT UNCIRCULATED   (often abbreviated to FDC, BU or B. Unc.). Coins in the finest possible condition, without any blemishes whatsoever.

UNCIRCULATED   (Unc) Modern machine-made coins are seldom found in FDC condition since they pick up minute scratches on their surfaces during production. Uncirculated is therefore the finest condition in which ordinary, non-proof coins are likely to be found. All details of the design are sharp and clear and the coin would still have its original lustre – the reddish tone found in shiny new pennies or cents or the silvery sparkle in new nickel or silver coins. With the passage of time this lustre tends to darken to an attractive patina. *Never* try to restore the original lustre by polishing the coin; such well-meaning action will destroy the collectable value of the coin.

EXTREMELY FINE   (EF) means a coin which still has all the detail in the design but has lost some or all of its original lustre as a result of having been in circulation to a limited extent.

VERY FINE   (VF) describes a coin in which the

Pennies in poor and extremely fine condition

very highest and finest points of the design are beginning to show some signs of wear. No modern coin should be collected in any grade less than VF, and as a rule dealers are not interested in purchasing coins in the lower grades. Nevertheless you may have examples in poorer condition as gap-fillers until a better specimen comes along. The lower grades are:

FINE (F) Such coins would show a fair amount of wear, the higher details of the design being blurred or smoothed away.

VERY GOOD (VG) A term which has become so debased that it now means pretty awful. Modern coins in VG condition are not worth bothering about, though often it is necessary to accept medieval and ancient coins in this state.

GOOD (G) indicates a coin which is worn all over, though the design would be legible and it would be just possible to make out the date. Below this grade are FAIR, MEDIOCRE and POOR which describe coins in worn and damaged condition, perhaps pierced with a hole, badly clipped, scratched or bent. Sometimes a coin will be found in Fine condition, but it has some blemish such as an edge knock (caused by dropping it on the floor); such a coin might still be collectable, although its value has suffered on account of this maltreatment.

An American money-box, 1885

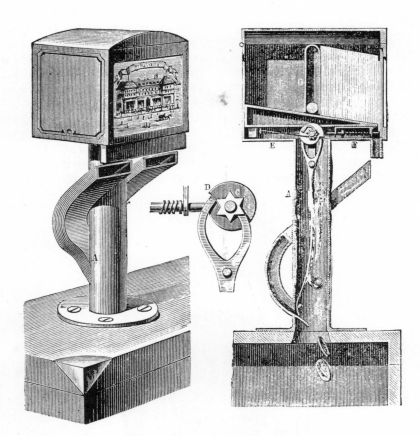

Facing Page Coin blank sorting machine which rejects any blanks over or under guage and diameter

15
THE CARE OF COINS AND TOKENS

If coins are worth collecting they are worth looking after. There are a few simple hints on the handling and care of coins. First and foremost, coins should not be handled more than is necessary. It is worth remembering that even the cleanest fingers have a thin film of sweat on them and a fingerprint on a coin is surprisingly difficult to remove. The acid in human sweat will tarnish the surface of the coin, severely affecting its appearance and value. Always handle coins by the rim, so that the minimum surface is actually touched by the fingers. Never rub a coin with the fingers, especially one in uncirculated condition, since this will disturb or remove the lustre.

Most coins, other than gold, darken in colour over the years. This darkening is known as patina and protects the surface of the coin from corrosion. Silver coins tend to turn black, while copper coins turn dark brown or greenish. This patina should be left untouched. Never attempt to polish coins to remove the patina and brighten them up. Once the original patina is lost the coin will tarnish and its value to the collector will be ruined. All forms of metal polish contain substances which rub or scratch the surface, and they should never be used. You might as well take a hammer and punch a hole in the coin as attempt to improve its appearance by polishing.

Although coins should never be polished it is sometimes advisable to clean them. There is a great difference between the natural patina and grease or dirt and it is quite acceptable to remove the latter. But great care must be taken to avoid scratching or damaging the surface in any way. Coins which are dirty or greasy may be cleaned by immersing them carefully in warm, soapy water and gently wiping them with a very soft cloth or cotton wool. A soft silver brush can sometimes be used – but again great care is needed. Methylated spirits or household ammonia can be used to clean silver coins. Copper and bronze coins are more susceptible to dirt and atmospheric pollution, but it is difficult to clean them satisfactorily and in most cases they are best left alone. If in doubt about cleaning, the best advice is – don't.

Nowadays the problem of looking after coins is solved by the fact that specimen sets are usually issued in plastic cases or folders and there is no need for the collector ever to take them out. Admittedly some of these plastic wallets are not very attractive to look at, and there is often a temptation to remove the coins. But once they have been taken out of their plastic envelope they can never be put back. These souvenir wallets,

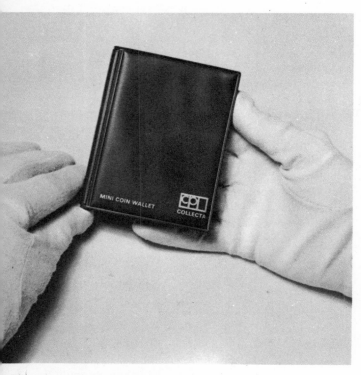

A pocket wallet for holding coins

folders and cases can be kept intact in shallow drawers or boxes.

Every collector, however, acquires loose coins and it is in housing them that the problems arise. Until recently the usual method of housing a coin collection was the wooden cabinet with shallow trays. The trays had a felt base and on top of this was a sheet of wood with holes cut out to correspond with the size of the coins. Cabinets are still used, but their disadvantages are that they take up a lot of room and are expensive. In addition, coins lying in the trays cannot be examined easily without being lifted out.

In recent years, however, coin albums have become very popular. They contain plastic sheets each with a number of pockets into which the coins are inserted. The advantages of the coin album are that it is relatively cheap, is very compact (several albums can be stacked together on a book-shelf), and both sides of the coin are readily seen without the coin having to be taken out of its pocket.

Another cheap, though less satisfactory, method is to place the coins one at a time into small manilla envelopes which can then be stored upright in long narrow boxes. The knife boxes used by jewellers and cutlers are ideal for this purpose. The details of the coin can be written on the outside of the envelope. The main disadvantage of this system is that the coins have to be removed from their envelopes every time they are examined.

The collecting of coins in sets according to their date and mint-mark developed in the United States and it was there, in the 1930s, that the coin folder was devised as an inexpensive means of housing date collections. The Whitman Coin Company of Racine, Wisconsin, pioneered the coin folder and this method has since been adopted all over the world. These folders are made of stout card and have holes punched out of them rather like the trays in coin cabinets. Each hole has a note stating the date or mint-mark of each major variety and all the collector has to do is to fit the coin into its appropriate hole. Folders of this sort are available for American and Canadian cents, nickels, dimes and quarters, British farthings, shillings, pennies and other coins, and a number of the more popular European coins where the run of different dates and mint-marks warrants it. As an added protection to the coins, and to prevent them from being dislodged, the folders are usually contained in a clear plastic sleeve, rather like a gramophone record, so that the coins are visible.

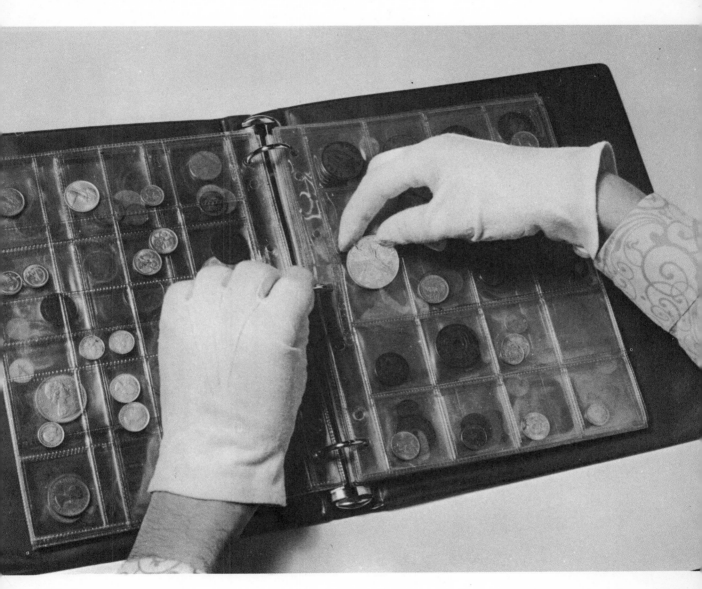

Inserting coins in an album.
The use of gloves is advisable
to avoid fingerprints on coin surfaces

CAPTIONS TO PICTURES IN CHAPTER HEADINGS

FRONTISPIECE Process of coining. (From a wood-cut engraved by order of the Emperor Maximillian)

Chapter 1 p.6 The Sphinx beside the pyramids, one of the wonders of the world

Chapter 2 p.10 The temple of Apollo at Sokia near Aidin in Anatolia (Modern Turkey)

Chapter 3 p. 16 Cirene. A ruined Graeco-Roman city in Cyrenaica, which flourished from 640 BC to 640AD

Chapter 3 p.17 A Roman road at Paestium

Chapter 4 p.24 *Two Tax Gatherers* by Marinus van Reymerswaele

Chapter 5 p.34 Top: Anglo-Saxon offering-pieces. Below: 18th century coining machinery

Chapter 6 p.50 The Bank of the United States of America in Philadelphia

Chapter 7 p.56 Lakatoi catamarans of Papua.

Chapter 8 p.68 In a money-lender's office, 1850

Chapter 9 p.78 Stone money from Yap Island, Western Pacific

Chapter 10 p.86 The death of Captain Cook at Onhyhee in the Sandwich Islands

Chapter 11 p.92 18th century tokens

Chapter 12 p. 101 Gaming tokens as used in the Wild West. *(Wild Rovers)*

Chapter 13 p.106 Making colonial coins at the Mint

Chapter 14 p.110 A tray from a coin cabinet. Note the correct method of handling coins

Chapter 15 p.118 Finished coins being inspected visually

ACKNOWLEDGEMENTS

The author and publishers are indebted to the following for the use of illustrative material in this book

Central Office of Information, Greek Embassy, Italian State Tourist Office, Mary Evans Picture Library, Metro-Goldwyn-Mayer, (Wild Rovers), *National Gallery, Public Records Office, Science Museum, Spink & Son Ltd., Twentieth Century Fox* (The Only Game in Town)

acing Page
doration of the Kings
etail) by Gossaert

Money-changers by David Teniers.

READING LIST

Below are listed a few of the more general works
on coins and tokens. In most cases they contain
reading lists giving details of more specialised
books on the various aspects of coin-collecting.

Coins

Carson, R. A. G.	*Coins, Ancient, Medieval and Modern*, 1970
Dowle, Anthony and Finn, Patrick	*Coins for Pleasure and Investment*, 1970
Hanson, T.	*Coin Collecting*, 1965
Hobson, Burton	*International Guide to Coin Collecting*, 1966
Laing, Lloyd R.	*Coins and Archaeology*, 1969
Linecar, Howard	*Beginner's Guide to Coin Collecting*, 1969
	An Advanced Guide to Coin Collecting, 1970
	Coin and Medal Collecting for Pleasure and Profit, 1971
	Coins and Medals, 1971
	Coins and Coin Collecting, 1971
Mackay, James	*Value in Coins and Medals*, 1968
	Coin Collecting for Grown-up Beginners, 1971
	Greek and Roman Coins, 1971
Mattingly, Harold	*Roman Coins*, 1962
Narbeth, Colin	*An Introduction to Coins and Medals*, 1970
Porteous, John	*Coins*, 1964
	Coins in History, 1969
Pridmore, F.	*The Coins of the British Commonwealth of Nations*
Purvey, Frank	*Collecting Coins*, 1963
Reinfeld, Fred	*Treasury of the World's Coins*, 1955
Seaby, B. A.	*Standard Catalogue of British Coins* (various editions)
Yeoman, R. S.	*Catalogue of Modern World Coins* (various editions)
	A Guide Book of United States Coins, 1964

Tokens

Bell, R. C.	*Tradesmen's Tickets and Private Tokens*, 1966
Dalton, R. and Hamer, S. H.	*The Provincial Token Coinage of the Eighteenth Century*, 1910
Davis, W. J. and Waters, A. W.	*Tickets and Passes of Great Britain and Ireland*, 1922
Mathias, P.	*English Trade Tokens*, 1962
Mishler, C.	*United States and Canadian Commemorative Medals and Tokens*, 1961
Waters, A. W.	*Notes on Eighteenth Century Tokens*, 1954
	Notes on Nineteenth Century Silver Tokens, 1957
Williamson, G. C.	*Trade Tokens issued in the Seventeenth Century in England, Wales and Ireland*, 1889

INDEX